Mir M Hossain

A PATH TO FREEDOM: THRIVING AS A MODERN

FREELANCER

By Mir M Hossain

#

Table of Contents

End   184

#

INTRODUCTION:

INTRODUCTION TO THE WORLD OF FREELANCING

As you embark on this journey through "Freelancing: A Path to Financial Freedom," I want to guide you into the world of freelancing, a realm brimming with potential for autonomy, professional growth, and, most importantly, financial independence. This is not just a career path; it's an opportunity for you to redefine your work and life on your own terms.

Understanding Freelancing:

Your New Career Approach: Freelancing means you offer your unique skills on a project basis, not tied down to a single employer. It's about embracing the role of a versatile, self-employed professional, juggling various projects and clients.

Diverse Opportunities Await You: Whatever your skill set – be it writing, programming, design, or consulting – freelancing offers a platform to showcase and monetize these talents.

Why You Should Choose Freelancing:

Master of Your Domain: The flexibility you gain in choosing when and where you work is unparalleled. This is about crafting a lifestyle as much as it is about a career.

Boundless Growth: Diverse projects mean diverse experiences, enriching your professional journey.

Unlock Your Earning Potential: Freelancing can lead to greater earnings than traditional employment, giving you a significant edge in your financial journey.

Tackling Freelancing Head-On:

Be Prepared for Income Variability: Brace yourself for fluctuating earnings – it's part and parcel of the freelance life. But remember, with risk comes reward.

You Are Your Own Boss: Ready yourself to handle everything from marketing to finances. It's a challenge, but it's also what makes the freelance life exhilarating.

Securing Your Future: You'll need to independently arrange for benefits like health insurance, but this also means tailored solutions that fit your specific needs.

Starting Your Freelance Journey:

Leverage Your Skills: Assess and polish your skills. This is your primary arsenal in the freelance market.

Build an Impressive Portfolio: Your portfolio is your professional voice. Make it resonate with potential clients.

Finding Clients: Use platforms dedicated to freelancing, network effectively, and let your social media profiles showcase your professional brand.

Prospering in the Freelance Economy:

Set the Right Price: Learn to value your work appropriately and negotiate confidently.

Know Your Rights and Responsibilities: Stay informed about legal aspects, from contracts to taxes.

Diverse Dreams: The Journey of a Modern Entrepreneur

Let's examine a true story, the personal journey of an entrepreneur, author and a freelancer Alex.

Alexr's journey is a rich tapestry of professional success and personal fulfillment. Born in a poor country, his path to success in the United States was marked by both academic and professional triumphs, including a master's degree and a thriving career in a multinational company.

Alex's journey is not just a tale of personal and professional triumph; it's a narrative enriched by his dedication to nurturing the potential in others. During his student life, Alex embarked on a path as a tutor, a role that transcended mere academic assistance. His unique approach to teaching, characterized by patience, inspiration, and a deep understanding

of individual student needs, left an indelible mark on those he

mentored.

Many of his students, influenced by his guidance and

wisdom, have since carved out successful paths in various

professional fields. This ripple effect of Alex's early tutoring days

is a testament to the profound impact a dedicated mentor can

have. His students, now flourishing in their careers, often

attribute their achievements to the foundational guidance they

received from Alex.

This dimension of Alex's story adds a layer of

communal contribution to his narrative. His success is not

measured solely by his entrepreneurial accomplishments or

sports trophies, but also by the success stories of those he

mentored. Alex's story, thus, becomes a beacon of inspiration, highlighting the power of knowledge-sharing and the lasting

influence of a committed educator.

In 2013, with a humble investment, ALEX launched

an Amazon venture that quickly grew into a million-dollar

enterprise. This success was not just a testament to his

business acumen but also to his philosophy that starting any

endeavor is half the battle won.

Beyond the world of business, ALEX was a

remarkable sportsman. He shined in local tournaments,

winning numerous trophies in tennis, chess, soccer, and other

sports. These achievements reflected his competitive spirit

and dedication, traits that also fueled his entrepreneurial

ventures.

ALEX's social nature and love for life played a

crucial role in his journey. He cherished the company of

friends and family, often seen as the life of gatherings. His

charismatic personality not only made him a beloved figure

in social circles but also helped him build a strong network

in the business world.

An avid traveler, ALEX loved to explore new places. His

travels were not just vacations; they were learning experiences

that broadened his perspective and inspired new ideas. This love

for exploration was evident in his willingness to venture into

unknown territories in business and philanthropy.

His books, filled with the wisdom gleaned from his

diverse experiences, encouraged readers to take the first step in

their endeavors. He emphasized the importance of willpower and

the courage to start, principles he lived by.

Balancing a demanding career, successful online

businesses, and a vibrant personal life, ALEX's story is a beacon of inspiration. It highlights that true success encompasses professional achievements, personal passions, and the joy of living life to the fullest.

As readers immerse in ALEX's story, they are reminded of the richness o f a balanced life. Success, as Alex demonstrated, is not just about financial gains or professional accolades; it's also about pursuing passions, nurturing relationships, and embracing the adventures life offers.

#

CHAPTER 1: THE FREELANCING LANDSCAPE

Understanding the Freelance Market

Understanding the freelance market is crucial for anyone looking to thrive in this growing sector. The freelance market, also known as the gig economy, encompasses a wide range of industries and skills, offering flexible work opportunities outside

the traditional employment model. Here's an overview to help

you navigate and understand this market:

1. Diversity of Opportunities

Industries: The freelance market spans various industries,

from writing, graphic design, and programming to consulting,

marketing, and more.

Skills: It values a wide array of skills, both technical and

creative. The demand for specific skills can vary based on

industry trends and technological advancements.

2. Market Trends

Growth: The freelance market has been growing rapidly,

accelerated by technological advancements and the increasing

acceptance of remote work.

Global Reach: Freelancers can work for clients from all

over the world, making this market highly globalized.

3. Platforms and Networking

Freelance Platforms: Websites like Upwork, Fiverr, and Freelancer connect freelancers with clients. They offer a structured way to find work, bid on projects, and build a portfolio.

Networking: Building a network through social media, professional contacts, and word-of-mouth is crucial for finding opportunities and growing your freelance business.

4. Pricing and Negotiation

Setting Rates: Freelancers set their rates based on experience, the complexity of the task, and market standards.

Negotiation Skills: Effective communication and negotiation skills are important for securing fair compensation and establishing clear project terms.

5. Challenges and Management

Inconsistent Income: Income can fluctuate, so financial management and planning are vital.

Self-Management: Freelancers need to manage their time, projects, and client relationships effectively.

6. Legal and Financial Aspects

Contracts: Clear contracts outlining project scope, deadlines, and payment terms are essential.

Taxes and Legalities: Understanding tax obligations and legal requirements in your region is crucial for compliance.

7. Continuous Learning and Adaptation

Skill Development: Staying updated with industry trends and continuously upgrading skills are important for remaining competitive.

Adaptability: Being adaptable and open to new opportunities and challenges is key in the dynamic freelance market.

8. Building a Personal Brand

Online Presence: A strong online presence through a personal website, social media, or a portfolio can attract clients.

Reputation: Building a good reputation through quality work and client testimonials can lead to more opportunities.

9. Work-Life Balance

Flexibility: Freelancing offers flexibility in work hours and location, but it's important to establish a healthy work-life balance.

Conclusion

The freelance market offers vast opportunities but also requires a strategic approach to navigate its challenges. Understanding the market dynamics, continuously developing skills, and building a strong network and personal brand are crucial for success in freelancing

Past, Present, and Future of Freelancing

Origins and Evolution of freelancing:

The origins and evolution of freelancing trace back to a rich history and have seen significant transformations over the years, adapting to societal and technological changes. Understanding this evolution provides context for today's freelancing landscape.

Historical Roots: The term "freelance" originates from the medieval mercenary knights who would fight for whoever paid them, hence they were 'free' lancers. This term was first recorded in Sir Walter Scott's novel "Ivanhoe".

Early Instances: In the arts and literary world, freelancing has been a practice for centuries. Notable historical figures like Leonardo da Vinci and William Shakespeare worked on a project basis, akin to modern freelancing.

Pre-Internet Era:

20th Century: Before the internet, freelancing was largely confined to certain professions like journalism, photography, and consulting. Freelancers found work through networking, word-of-mouth, and local advertising.

Challenges: Freelancers faced limitations in terms of reach and client base, often working within local or regional markets. Communication and project management were also more challenging without digital tools.

Digital Revolution

Internet Impact: The advent of the internet revolutionized freelancing. It expanded the market beyond local boundaries, enabling freelancers to connect with clients globally.

Online Platforms: Websites like Upwork, Fiverr, and Freelancer emerged, creating structured marketplaces where freelancers could find work and manage projects across various fields.

Historically, the term "freelance" first appeared in Sir Walter Scott's novel "Ivanhoe" to describe a medieval mercenary.

Quote: **"Choose a job you love, and you will never have to work a day in your life**." - **Confucius.**

Freelancing is not a new term , it always existed with different forms and terms.

This ancient wisdom encapsulates the freelance ethos of pursuing passion-based work.

Renowned writers like Ernest Hemingway and Mark Twain started as freelancers, often facing the challenges of inconsistent work and the need for extensive self-promotion.

Present/Modern day freelancing

Technology-Driven Growth:

The Technology-Driven Growth of Freelancing is a key aspect of how the freelance market has evolved and continues to evolve. This growth is largely fueled by advancements in technology that have significantly changed the way freelancers work, find jobs, and interact with clients. Here are some key points highlighting this growth:

1. Digital Platforms and Marketplaces

Online Freelance Platforms: Websites like Upwork, Fiverr, and Freelancer have revolutionized freelancing. They provide a platform where freelancers can showcase their skills, connect with clients globally, and manage projects. These platforms have made it easier for freelancers to find work and for clients to find skilled professionals.

Fact: As of my last update in April 2023, Upwork reported millions of registered freelancers and clients, illustrating the expansive reach of these platforms.

2. Remote Collaboration Tools

Communication and Collaboration: Tools like Zoom, Slack, and Trello have become integral for freelancers. They facilitate effective communication and project management, making it easier to work with clients and teams from anywhere in the world.

Impact: These tools have made remote work more feasible and efficient, helping freelancers to collaborate on projects seamlessly despite geographical differences.

3. Mobile Technologies

On-the-Go Working: Smartphones and mobile applications allow freelancers to work, communicate with clients, and manage their business from anywhere. This mobility has contributed significantly to the flexibility and appeal of freelancing.

Example: Many freelancers use mobile apps for time tracking, invoicing, and even for performing their actual work, like graphic design or writing.

4. Cloud Computing

Data Storage and Accessibility: Cloud services like Google Drive and Dropbox offer freelancers a way to store and access their work from any device, enhancing flexibility and security.

Collaboration: Cloud computing also enables real-time collaboration on documents and projects, streamlining workflow and project management.

5. Social Media and Networking

Building Online Presence: Social media platforms like LinkedIn, Twitter, and Instagram have become powerful tools for freelancers to network, market their services, and build their personal brand.

Client Acquisition: Freelancers often use these platforms to share their work, connect with potential clients, and stay updated with industry trends.

6. Specialized Software and Tools

Industry-Specific Tools: The availability of specialized software for different fields, such as graphic design, video editing, or coding, has empowered freelancers to deliver professional-grade services.

Automation: Tools that automate certain tasks, like invoicing or scheduling, free up time for freelancers to focus on their core work.

7. Security and Payment Technologies

Secure Transactions: Advancements in payment technologies and platforms ensure secure and efficient transactions, crucial for freelancers who often work with international clients.

Cryptocurrencies and Blockchain: Emerging technologies like blockchain and cryptocurrencies might further revolutionize how freelancers receive payments, offering more security and potentially lower transaction fees.

The technology-driven growth of freelancing has significantly lowered entry barriers, enabling more people to participate in the gig economy. It has also enhanced the efficiency, reach, and scalability of freelance work. As technology continues to advance, it is likely to bring even more transformative changes to the world of freelancing. As of my last update in 2023, platforms like Upwork and Fiverr had millions of registered users, showcasing the massive scale of the freelance economy.

Quote: "**The way to get started is to quit talking and begin doing**." - Walt Disney. This reflects the action-oriented approach of modern freelancers.

Diverse Opportunities:

Explore industries that align with your passions and skills to find fulfilling freelance work. For instance, renowned photographer Annie Leibovitz started her career freelancing,

transforming her passion for photography into a successful career.

To dive into creative fields like photography or graphic design,

platforms like **Behance and Dribbble** are excellent for

showcasing portfolios and finding work.

In technical fields like web development or software

engineering, consider following the path of individuals like Linus

Torvalds, who began his journey with freelance projects before

creating Linux. **GitHub and Stack Overflow** are essential for

showcasing coding skills and collaborating on projects.

For those inclined towards marketing and business, take

inspiration from Gary Vaynerchuk, who partly built his business

empire through freelance consulting. LinkedIn is a powerful tool

for networking and finding opportunities in these areas.

If education and training are your interests, look at the example of Salman Khan, who started Khan Academy initially as a tutoring project. Platforms like **Udemy and Coursera** are great resources for creating and selling educational courses.

For entry-level freelancers, consider starting with tasks like data entry or basic research. Many virtual assistants begin their careers with these kinds of tasks. Websites like **FlexJobs** and **Upwork** offer a variety of entry-level opportunities.

For those with more experience, seeking expert-level projects can be highly rewarding. Experienced professionals, akin to consultants from McKinsey & Company, often engage in freelance consulting. **Toptal** is a platform that caters to high-skilled freelancers, offering opportunities for complex and well-paying projects.

Embrace the flexibility and customization that freelancing offers. Mark Manson, for instance, started with a specific niche in blogging and developed it into a full-time career. To explore niche markets, WordPress and Medium are excellent resources for starting a blog or publishing articles.

The global reach of freelancing allows you to work with international clients, much like many freelance translators do. **ProZ.com** is a great platform for those looking to offer translation services to a global clientele.

Stay updated and evolve with emerging fields like blockchain technology. Freelancers working in this area, such as Ethereum developers, are in high demand. **CryptoJobsLis**t is an ideal resource for finding blockchain-related freelance jobs.

Lastly, continuous learning is crucial. Sites like Coursera and LinkedIn Learning offer courses to help you stay abreast of the latest industry trends and develop new skills.

By following these paths and utilizing the recommended resources, you can navigate the diverse opportunities in freelancing and build a fulfilling and successful careeThe diverse opportunities in freelancing make it an attractive and viable career path for many individuals. This diversity not only caters to a wide range of skills and interests but also encourages continuous growth and adaptation in an ever-changing job market. Whether someone is looking for creative freedom, technical challenges, or entrepreneurial ventures, freelancing offers a unique and flexible way to achieve professional and personal goals

Future of freelance

Market Predictions:

Fact: A study by Upwork predicted that freelancers could make up the majority of the U.S. workforce by 2027, indicating significant growth potential.

Quote: "The best way to predict the future is to create it." - Peter Drucker. This is especially relevant for freelancers who shape their career paths.

Workplace Integration:

Example: Companies like Google and Microsoft increasingly rely on freelancers for specialized projects, showcasing a trend towards hybrid workforce models.

Economic Impact:

Fact: Freelancers contribute billions to the economy annually, with their impact expected to increase as the gig economy grows.

Challenges and Adaptation:

Quote: "Adaptability is about the powerful difference between adapting to cope and adapting to win." - Max McKeown. This highlights the need for freelancers to continuously evolve their skills.

Niche Specialization:

Example: Freelancers in emerging fields like AI and blockchain are already commanding high rates due to their specialized skills.

Global Collaboration: With the rise of digital communication tools, freelancers are increasingly working in global teams, breaking down geographical barriers.

Statistics and Trends in Freelancing

As of my last update in April 2023, the freelancing landscape was characterized by significant growth and evolving trends. These developments are reflected in various statistics that highlight the expanding role of freelancing in the global workforce. Here are some key statistics and trends:

Key Statistics

Workforce Composition:

A significant portion of the global workforce is engaged in freelancing. For example, in the United States, freelancers were predicted by some studies to become the majority of the workforce by 2027.

In Europe, countries like the Netherlands and the UK have also seen a substantial rise in the number of freelancers.

Economic Contribution:

Freelancers contribute billions to the economy. In the U.S. alone, freelancers were contributing over $1 trillion annually to the economy, a figure that has likely grown.

Demographic Diversity:

The demographic of freelancers is diverse, spanning various age groups, with a notable presence of both millennials and Gen Z, indicating a generational shift towards freelance work.

There's also a growing trend of mid-career and senior professionals transitioning to freelancing.

Current Trends

Technology Integration:

Advancements in technology, especially in communication and project management tools, continue to facilitate remote and flexible working arrangements for freelancers.

Rise of Digital Nomadism:

There's an increasing trend of digital nomadism, where freelancers combine work and travel, leveraging the flexibility of their work arrangements.

Diversification of Skills:

Freelancers are diversifying their skill sets to cater to a broader range of services, driven partly by the evolving demands of the digital economy.

Gig Economy Platforms:

The growth of platforms like Upwork, Fiverr, and Freelancer.com continues, with these platforms expanding their services and user base.

Freelancers in Specialized Fields:

There is a growing demand for freelancers in specialized fields such as AI, blockchain, and cybersecurity, reflecting broader technological trends.

Impact of Economic Fluctuations:

Economic uncertainties often lead to an increase in freelance work, as companies prefer hiring freelancers for flexibility and cost-effectiveness during fluctuating market conditions.

Policy and Legal Changes:

As freelancing becomes more prevalent, there's an increasing focus on policies and legal frameworks to better protect the rights and interests of freelancers.

Future Outlook

The future of freelancing is expected to see continued growth, with more individuals embracing freelance work for its flexibility, potential for higher earnings, and work-life balance.

The gig economy is also anticipated to play a critical role in shaping labor markets and influencing employment policies globally.

These statistics and trends underscore the dynamic nature of freelancing, highlighting its increasing importance in the modern workforce and its potential to shape future work practices.

Conclusion

The trajectory of freelancing, from its humble beginnings to its current prominence and future potential, is a testament to the evolving nature of work. By embracing change, continually adapting skills, and leveraging technology, freelancers are well-positioned to thrive in this dynamic landscape

CHAPTER 2: IS FREELANCING RIGHT FOR YOU?

Self-Assessment: Skills, Temperament, and Goals

Embarking on a freelancing career requires a thorough self-assessment to ensure you're well-equipped for the challenges and opportunities it presents. Evaluating your skills, temperament, and goals is crucial to succeed in this increasingly competitive field. Here's how you can approach this self-assessment:

Assessing Skills

Identify Your Core Skills: Reflect on what you are good at. Are you a great writer, a skilled programmer, or an effective marketer? Your core skills are your primary offering as a freelancer.

Market Demand: Research the market demand for your skills. Some skills might be in high demand, while others might be more niche.

Skill Gaps: Honestly assess if there are gaps in your skill set that need to be addressed through training or practice.

Evaluating Temperament

Self-Motivation: Freelancing requires a high degree of self-motivation. You need to be able to push yourself to find clients, meet deadlines, and manage projects.

Adaptability: The freelance market can be volatile. Assess your ability to adapt to changing market conditions and client demands.

Stress Management: Evaluate how well you handle stress and uncertainty. Freelancing can have unpredictable income and workloads.

Setting Goals

Short-term Goals: Define what you want to achieve in the next few months. It could be landing your first client, earning a certain amount, or completing a specific number of projects.

Long-term Goals: Consider where you want your freelance career to be in the next few years. Do you want to establish a steady client base, expand into new markets, or build your brand?

Personal Goals: Freelancing should align with your personal goals. Whether it's having more flexibility, pursuing a passion, or achieving a better work-life balance.

Practical Steps for Self-Assessment

SWOT Analysis: Conduct a SWOT analysis (Strengths, Weaknesses, Opportunities, Threats) to get a clear picture of where you stand.

Seek Feedback: Get feedback from peers, mentors, or previous employers to understand your strengths and areas for improvement.

Professional Development: Identify courses, workshops, or other training programs that can help you enhance your skills.

Financial Assessment: Ensure you understand the financial implications of freelancing, such as irregular income streams and the need for self-funding benefits.

Mindset Preparation: Prepare yourself mentally for the freelance lifestyle. It's different from a regular 9-to-5 job and requires a significant shift in mindset.

Conclusion

A thorough self-assessment is the foundation of a successful freelancing career. It helps you understand your capabilities, prepare for the challenges ahead, and set realistic and achievable goals. Remember, freelancing is a journey of continuous learning and adaptation, so your self-assessment should be an ongoing process.

The Myths and Realities of Freelancing

Freelancing often comes with many myths and misconceptions. Understanding the realities can help set appropriate expectations and strategies for success. Here's a look at some common myths and the actual realities of freelancing:

Myth 1: Freelancers Have a Lot of Free Time

Reality: While freelancers do have flexible schedules, this often translates to irregular work hours. Many freelancers work long hours, including weekends, to meet deadlines or manage client demands. Time management becomes a crucial skill for freelancers.

Myth 2: Freelancing Is an Easy Way to Make Money

Reality: Freelancing can indeed be lucrative, but it's not necessarily easy. Success in freelancing often requires consistent effort in finding clients, marketing oneself, honing skills, and delivering quality work. The income can also be unpredictable, especially in the early stages.

Myth 3: Freelancers Work from Anywhere, So It's Always Fun

Reality: While freelancing offers the flexibility to work from different locations, it's not always a leisurely endeavor. Working from cafes or while traveling sounds appealing, but it requires discipline and good working conditions, like reliable internet and a conducive work environment.

Myth 4: Freelancing Is Less Stressful Than a Regular Job

Reality: Freelancing can bring its own set of stresses, like fluctuating income, client acquisition, and project deadlines. Unlike regular jobs, freelancers don't have the same level of job security or benefits like health insurance, which can add to the stress.

Myth 5: Freelancers Are Always Working Alone

Reality: While freelancing does involve a significant amount of solo work, successful freelancers often collaborate with other freelancers, form networks, and may even build teams as their business grows. Communication and networking skills are key in the freelance world.

Myth 6: Freelancing Is Only for Creative Professions

Reality: Freelancing spans a wide range of industries beyond creative fields. It includes sectors like IT, consulting, marketing, education, and many others. The digital age has opened up freelancing opportunities in numerous non-traditional fields.

Myth 7: It's a Temporary or Part-Time Endeavor

Reality: For many, freelancing is a full-time career and a long-term choice. With the growth of the gig economy, many professionals are choosing freelancing for its flexibility, autonomy, and potential for growth, making it a sustainable career option.

Conclusion

Understanding these myths and realities is crucial for anyone considering a freelance career. It requires a blend of skill, dedication, and adaptability. Being aware of these aspects can help aspiring freelancers prepare better and set realistic expectations for their freelance journey.

Inspirational Stories from Successful Freelancers

Let's look at a real-life success story from the world of freelancing:

The Story of Jon Morrow

Background: Jon Morrow is a blogger, writer, and entrepreneur who has achieved remarkable success in the world of online writing and blogging. His journey is particularly inspiring because he has done this while overcoming significant personal challenges.

Challenges:

Jon was born with Spinal Muscular Atrophy, a disease that leaves him unable to move any part of his body except his face. Despite this, he refused to let his physical limitations define his life or career.

Career Journey:

Jon began his freelance journey as a writer and blogger. He worked for sites like Copyblogger and KISSmetrics, building a reputation for his compelling writing and marketing insights.

One of his significant early successes was at Copyblogger, where he became the Associate Editor and helped grow the blog's audience significantly.

Success:

Jon founded Smart Blogger, a website dedicated to teaching people how to write better content and grow their audience online. Under his guidance, Smart Blogger has become a go-to resource for aspiring bloggers and writers.

Despite his physical limitations, Jon uses voice recognition software to write his content. He has built a successful business that earns him millions of dollars.

Key Achievements:

Jon's blog posts have been viewed by millions of people. He has a large following on social media and a successful email list that's central to his business model.

He has helped numerous individuals and businesses improve their content writing and marketing strategies.

Lessons:

Jon's story is a testament to perseverance, resilience, and the power of leveraging one's skills and passion, regardless of physical limitations.

He demonstrates the potential of digital platforms to build a successful and impactful career, showcasing how determination and adaptability can overcome significant challenges.

Conclusion

Jon Morrow's story is not just an inspiration to freelancers but to anyone facing obstacles in their career. It highlights the opportunities that the digital age offers for creating a successful and fulfilling career, regardless of personal circumstances. His success underscores the importance of skill, passion, and resilience in the freelancing world.

Here are five real-life inspirational stories from the world of freelancing:

1. Hanny Kusumawati: From Freelancer to Entrepreneur

Background: Hanny, an Indonesian writer and blogger, started as a freelance writer.

Journey: She co-founded Coin A Chance!, a movement to help underprivileged children, and later established a creative consultancy firm.

Success: Hanny's firm, Beradadisini, focuses on content creation, personal branding, and digital storytelling, serving clients globally.

Lesson: Hanny's story shows how freelancing can evolve into social entrepreneurship and impactful business ventures.

2. Kat Boogaard: Freelance Writing Success

Background: Kat began her career in a traditional 9-to-5 job but transitioned to freelance writing.

Journey: She faced initial challenges in building a client base but persisted in honing her writing skills.

Success: Kat is now a successful freelance writer featured in numerous publications and runs a blog offering advice to aspiring freelancers.

Lesson: Her story exemplifies the potential for a successful freelance career through persistence and skill development.

3. Tom Ewer: Creating a Lucrative Freelance Writing Business

Background: Tom started as a blogger and freelance writer.

Journey: He founded Leaving Work Behind, a blog sharing his freelance journey and tips for success.

Success: He grew his blog into a full-fledged business, offering freelance writing services and consulting.

Lesson: Tom's experience demonstrates how personal branding and blogging can be leveraged to build a lucrative freelance business.

4. Danny Margulies: Freelancer to Six-Figure Copywriter

Background: Danny started freelancing with no prior experience in copywriting.

Journey: He learned and applied skills in copywriting and freelancing, using platforms like Upwork.

Success: Danny now earns a six-figure income and runs a successful blog teaching others how to succeed in freelancing.

Lesson: His story shows that with the right learning and strategies, even beginners can achieve great success in freelancing.

5. Morgan Overholt: Graphic Designer Turned Millionaire

Background: Morgan worked as a graphic designer for various companies but felt unfulfilled.

Journey: She decided to freelance full-time, despite initial financial struggles.

Success: Morgan's freelance business grew rapidly, and she now runs a multimillion-dollar graphic design firm.

Lesson: Her journey highlights the potential for freelancers to grow their individual skills into profitable businesses.

These stories of freelancers from diverse backgrounds and industries illustrate the vast potential of freelancing. They show how dedication, skill development, and strategic thinking can lead to remarkable success and personal fulfillment.

CHAPTER 3: SETTING THE FOUNDATION

Building a Freelancing Mindset

Building a successful freelancing career requires more than just skills and opportunities; it demands a specific mindset. A freelancing mindset is a blend of various attitudes and perspectives that help you navigate the unique challenges and opportunities of freelance work. Here are key elements to develop and nurture this mindset:

1. Adaptability

Embrace Change: Freelancing is dynamic, with fluctuating workloads, changing client needs, and evolving market trends. Being adaptable allows you to thrive in this ever-changing environment.

Continuous Learning: Stay updated with industry trends and continuously develop your skills.

2. Self-Motivation and Discipline

Goal-Setting: Set clear, achievable goals to keep yourself focused and motivated.

Routine and Structure: Establish a daily routine and create a dedicated workspace to instill discipline, even in a flexible work environment.

3. Resilience

Handle Rejection: Understand that rejection and criticism are part of the journey. Use them as learning opportunities to grow.

Stay Persistent: Success in freelancing often requires persistence through challenging times.

4. Financial Savvy

Plan Financially: Learn to manage irregular income streams. This includes budgeting, saving for lean periods, and investing wisely.

Understand Your Worth: Know the value of your work and learn to negotiate effectively with clients.

5. Networking and Relationship Building

Build Connections: Networking is crucial in freelancing for finding work and support. Cultivate relationships with clients and peers.

Effective Communication: Honing your communication skills helps in managing client expectations and resolving issues.

6. Problem-Solving Attitude

Innovative Solutions: Be prepared to tackle challenges head-on and find creative solutions.

Decision-Making: Develop the ability to make informed decisions quickly and efficiently.

7. Work-Life Balance

Set Boundaries: It's important to balance work with personal life. Set boundaries to ensure you have time for rest and leisure.

Self-Care: Prioritize your health and well-being to maintain productivity and creativity.

8. Professional Development

Seek Feedback: Regularly seek and learn from feedback to improve your services.

Professional Growth: Invest in your professional development through courses, workshops, and other learning opportunities.

Conclusion

Developing a freelancing mindset is a journey in itself. It involves cultivating qualities that not only help you manage the practical aspects of freelancing but also contribute to personal growth and satisfaction. By nurturing these attributes, you can build a resilient, adaptable, and successful freelancing career.Essential Skills for Freelancers

Time Management and Organizational Strategies

Effective time management and organizational strategies are crucial for freelancers, who often juggle multiple projects and clients. Without a structured approach, it's easy to become overwhelmed and unproductive. Here are some strategies to help manage your time and stay organized:

1. Prioritize Tasks

Identify Urgent vs. Important: Use tools like the Eisenhower Box to distinguish between tasks that are urgent, important, both, or neither.

Focus on High-Impact Activities: Concentrate on tasks that will have the most significant impact on your goals.

2. Use a Planner or Digital Calendar

Schedule Everything: Block out time for work tasks, meetings, and even breaks. Tools like Google Calendar can be effective for this.

Set Reminders: Utilize reminders to keep track of deadlines and upcoming meetings.

3. Set Realistic Deadlines

Allocate Extra Time: Give yourself a buffer by setting deadlines a few days before the actual due date to accommodate any unforeseen delays.

Communicate with Clients: Be transparent with clients about how long tasks will realistically take.

4. Break Down Large Projects

Small, Manageable Tasks: Divide big projects into smaller tasks. This makes them less daunting and easier to tackle.

Use Project Management Tools: Tools like Trello or Asana can help manage and track progress.

5. Eliminate Distractions

Dedicated Workspace: Have a designated area for work to separate professional and personal life.

Limit Interruptions: Use techniques like the Pomodoro Technique to focus for specific periods and take short breaks.

6. Batch Similar Tasks

Task Batching: Group similar tasks together to complete them more efficiently. For example, allocate a specific time for all your email correspondence.

7. Regular Reviews and Adjustments

Weekly Reviews: At the end of each week, review what you've accomplished and plan for the next week.

Adjust Strategies: Be flexible and willing to adjust your methods if certain strategies aren't working.

8. Set Boundaries

Client Expectations: Communicate your working hours to clients to set clear boundaries.

Learn to Say No: Don't overcommit. It's okay to turn down work if it doesn't fit into your schedule or align with your goals.

9. Stay Physically and Mentally Healthy

Regular Breaks: Take breaks to avoid burnout. Short walks or exercise can rejuvenate your mind.

Healthy Lifestyle: A healthy diet and adequate sleep can significantly impact productivity.

Conclusion

Time management and organization are skills that can be developed and refined over time. By implementing these strategies, freelancers can work more efficiently, meet deadlines, and maintain a healthy work-life balance, ultimately leading to greater satisfaction and success in their freelance careers.

#

CHAPTER 4: LAUNCHING YOUR FREELANCE CAREER

Creating Your Brand and Online Presence

Strong branding is not just a superficial layer; it's a fundamental aspect of your professional identity that can significantly influence how clients perceive and interact with you. Here's the revised response with added emphasis on the importance of branding and real-life examples:

Crucial Importance of Branding

Creating a powerful brand and online presence is not just beneficial but essential for freelancers. It's the cornerstone of how you are perceived in the marketplace. A well-crafted brand can set you apart, build trust, and communicate your value proposition effectively.

1. Define Your Brand - Essential for Differentiation

Unique Value Proposition: Identify what sets you apart from the competition. This uniqueness in your services or approach is what will make you memorable in the minds of clients.

Consistent Brand Identity: Choose elements like a logo and color scheme that reflect your professional image and use them consistently across all platforms. This consistency helps in building brand recognition.

2. Build a Professional Website - Your Digital Storefront

Portfolio Showcasing: Your website is often the first point of contact with potential clients. A well-organized portfolio demonstrates your skills and professionalism.

Testimonials for Trust: Client testimonials add credibility and give prospects a sense of security about your reliability and quality of work.

3. Leverage Social Media - Expanding Your Reach

Strategic Platform Choice: Different platforms serve different purposes. Choose the ones that align best with your target audience and area of expertise.

Engagement and Visibility: Regular posts and interactions on social media keep you top of mind for potential clients.

4. Content Marketing - Establish Authority

Blogging or Vlogging: By sharing expert insights, you position yourself as an authority in your field. This is critical in building a trusted brand.

SEO for Visibility: Effective SEO strategies enhance your online presence, making it easier for potential clients to find you.

5. Networking and Collaborations - Building Relationships

Online Networking: Engaging with others in your industry online can lead to referrals and collaborative opportunities.

Collaborations for Growth: Working with others can expand your reach and add to your brand's credibility.

6. Online Reviews and Reputation - Managing Perceptions

Importance of Reviews: Positive reviews significantly enhance your brand's trustworthiness.

Reputation Management: Actively managing your online reputation is crucial in maintaining a positive brand image.

7. Email Marketing - Personalized Engagement

Email List as an Asset: An email list allows for direct and personalized communication with your audience, enhancing your brand's personal connection with clients.

Regular Updates to Stay Relevant: Keeping your audience informed and engaged helps in building a loyal client base.

8. Consistency Across All Touchpoints

Unified Brand Experience: Ensure every interaction with your brand, from your social media posts to your business cards, communicates a consistent message.

Real-Life Examples

Marie Forleo: Marie's brand as a life coach and motivational speaker is a prime example. Her consistent branding across her website, social media, and YouTube channel has established her as a leading figure in her field.

Gary Vaynerchuk: Gary's brand is built on his unique style and approach to marketing and entrepreneurship. His consistent branding across various platforms has made him a household name in the business world.

Conclusion

In the freelance market, where competition is fierce, a strong brand can be the difference between being overlooked and being sought after. It's about creating a memorable identity that resonates with your target audience. Successful freelancers understand this and invest time and resources in building and maintaining a strong brand.

Finding and Securing Your First Clients

Securing your first clients as a freelancer can be one of the most challenging yet rewarding steps in your career. It requires a combination of strategy, persistence, and effective marketing. Here's a guide to help you find and secure your initial clients:

1. Identify Your Target Market

Understand who needs your services and where you can find them. This could involve defining the industries, business sizes, or even geographic locations that best fit your skill set.

2. Leverage Your Network

Start with your existing connections. Let your friends, family, and former colleagues know about your freelancing services. Personal referrals can often lead to your first clients.

3. Create a Strong Portfolio

Showcase your best work to demonstrate your skills and expertise. If you don't have client work to show yet, consider creating mock projects or volunteering your services to non-profits to build your portfolio.

4. Use Freelance Platforms

Platforms like Upwork, Freelancer, and Fiverr can be good starting points. Create detailed profiles showcasing your skills and bid on relevant projects.

5. Engage on Social Media and Forums

Join and participate in industry-specific groups on LinkedIn, Reddit, or Facebook. Sharing your knowledge and engaging in discussions can attract potential clients.

6. Content Marketing and Blogging

Start a blog related to your field. Sharing valuable insights and information can attract clients and establish you as an expert in your field.

7. Cold Emailing and Outreach

Identify potential clients and reach out to them with personalized emails. Highlight how your services can solve specific problems they might have.

8. Attend Networking Events

Join local or online networking events and workshops relevant to your industry. Networking can often lead to unexpected opportunities.

9. Offer an Introductory Discount

Consider offering a discount or a special package to your first few clients. This can be a way to encourage them to take a chance on a new freelancer.

10. Collect Testimonials

Once you complete a project, ask your client for a testimonial. Positive reviews can be powerful tools for attracting more clients.

11. Referral Program

Implement a referral program where existing clients get a benefit for referring new clients to you. Word-of-mouth can be a powerful marketing tool.

12. Be Persistent and Patient

Finding your first clients can take time. Stay persistent in your marketing efforts and keep improving your skills.

Real-Life Example

Pete Kistler: He struggled to find employment due to a case of mistaken identity on Google. This challenge led him to learn about SEO and online reputation management, eventually co-founding BrandYourself. He started by offering his services to those with similar issues, gradually expanding his client base through referrals and effective online marketing.

Conclusion

Securing your first clients requires a mix of proactive outreach, building a strong online presence, and utilizing your network. It's important to be patient and persistent, as building a client base takes time and consistent effort. Once you secure your first few clients, focus on delivering excellent work to build a reputation that will attract more clients.

Establishing a Portfolio

Establishing a strong portfolio is a key step in launching a successful freelancing career. It serves as a visual representation of your skills, experience, and professionalism. Here's how you can build an effective portfolio:

1. Select Your Best Work

Choose pieces that showcase your skills and range of expertise. It's better to have a few high-quality samples than many mediocre ones.

2. Diversify Your Portfolio

Include a variety of work that demonstrates your versatility, but also make sure it's relevant to the services you offer.

3. Create Detailed Descriptions

For each piece, include a brief description that explains the project, your role, the skills you used, and the outcome or impact of your work.

4. Showcase Outcomes and Achievements

Where possible, include results or successes from your projects, like increased website traffic or improved sales figures, to demonstrate the effectiveness of your work.

5. Keep Your Portfolio Updated

Regularly update your portfolio with new work to keep it current and show prospective clients that you're active in your field.

6. Use Professional Presentation

Ensure your portfolio is well-organized and presented in a professional format. An aesthetically pleasing and easy-to-navigate portfolio can make a strong impression.

7. Include Client Testimonials

If you have positive feedback from clients, include these testimonials in your portfolio. They add credibility and give potential clients insight into working with you.

8. Make Your Portfolio Easily Accessible

Your portfolio should be easy to find and access. Consider creating a dedicated section on your website or use platforms like Behance for creative work.

9. Tailor Your Portfolio for Your Audience

Customize your portfolio based on the client or job you're targeting. Highlight work that's most relevant to their specific needs or industry.

10. Personal Projects Matter

If you're new to freelancing and don't have client work to show, include personal projects. They can be just as effective in showcasing your skills and creativity.

11. Online and Offline Versions

Have both online and printable versions of your portfolio. Some clients may prefer a physical copy, especially if you're attending in-person meetings.

12. Include Your Contact Information

Make sure your portfolio has clear contact information, making it easy for potential clients to reach out to you.

Conclusion

A well-crafted portfolio is more than just a collection of your work; it's a tool to communicate your expertise and the value you can bring to potential clients. It should evolve with

your career, showcasing your growth and success as a freelancer.

#

CHAPTER 5: MASTERING THE ART OF NETWORKING

Building Professional Relationships

Building strong professional relationships is a critical aspect of a successful freelancing career. These relationships not only help in securing continuous work but also in expanding your network and gaining referrals. Here's how you can build and maintain professional relationships in the freelancing world:

1. Deliver Quality Work Consistently

The foundation of good professional relationships is consistently delivering high-quality work. Meeting or exceeding client expectations can lead to repeat business and referrals.

2. Effective Communication

Regular and clear communication is key. Keep your clients updated on project progress and be responsive to their inquiries and feedback.

3. Understand Your Client's Needs

Take time to understand what each client really needs. Tailoring your approach to their specific requirements can make them feel valued and strengthen the relationship.

4. Be Reliable and Meet Deadlines

Reliability builds trust. Always strive to meet deadlines, and if you foresee a delay, communicate it as soon as possible.

5. Seek Feedback and Act on It

After completing a project, ask for feedback. This shows that you're committed to continuous improvement and value their opinion.

6. Networking Events and Industry Meetups

Attend industry events, workshops, and meetups to connect with potential clients and fellow freelancers. Face-to-face interactions can be very effective for building lasting relationships.

7. Use Social Media to Stay in Touch

Platforms like LinkedIn are great for maintaining professional relationships. Regularly share updates about your work and engage with your connections' content.

8. Collaborate with Other Freelancers

Collaborations can lead to mutual referrals and shared projects. Building relationships with other freelancers can open up opportunities you might not have access to on your own.

9. Follow Up Regularly

Periodically check in with past clients to keep the relationship alive. A simple email asking how they are doing can keep you on their radar for future projects.

10. Show Appreciation

Acknowledge and thank your clients for their business. A thank you note or a small gesture of appreciation can go a long way.

11. Join Online Communities and Forums

Participate in online communities related to your field. Share your knowledge, answer questions, and engage in discussions.

12. Offer Help Beyond Your Services

Sometimes, you can offer advice or help that may not directly relate to your services. This can build goodwill and a sense of partnership.

Real-Life Example

Jane, a Freelance Graphic Designer: She maintained strong relationships with her clients by providing exceptional designs and being proactive in her communications. She regularly attended local business networking events, which not only helped her gain new clients but also connect with other freelancers. Through LinkedIn, she kept in touch with her professional network, sharing updates about her projects and engaging with posts by others. This approach helped her in gaining repeat business and valuable referrals.

Conclusion

Building professional relationships in freelancing is about more than just networking; it's about creating trust, adding value, and maintaining connections. These relationships are essential for a sustainable and growing freelance career.

Networking Strategies and Platforms

Effective networking is a vital component of a successful freelancing career. It's not just about meeting new people; it's about building connections that can lead to opportunities, collaborations, and growth. Here are strategies and platforms that can help you network effectively as a freelancer:

Networking Strategies

Identify Your Goals: Understand what you want to achieve through networking, whether it's finding clients, learning from peers, or building collaborations.

Be Genuine: Authenticity is key. Show genuine interest in the people you meet. Networking is about building relationships, not just exchanging business cards.

Offer Value: Approach networking with a mindset of what you can offer. This could be your expertise, advice, or connections. People are more likely to remember and help those who've helped them.

Prepare an Elevator Pitch: Have a concise and compelling way to describe what you do. This makes it easier to engage in conversations at networking events.

Follow Up: After meeting someone, follow up with a personalized message. Mention something specific from your conversation to show that you were attentive.

Stay in Touch: Regularly check in with your contacts. You can share relevant articles, congratulate them on professional achievements, or just drop a friendly note.

Volunteer or Speak at Events: Offering your time or expertise at events can increase your visibility and establish you as an authority in your field.

Networking Platforms

LinkedIn: Ideal for professional networking, LinkedIn allows you to connect with industry professionals, join groups, share content, and discover networking events.

Meetup: This platform has groups for almost every industry and interest, providing opportunities to attend local events and meet like-minded professionals.

Twitter: Great for following industry leaders and engaging in conversations through hashtags relevant to your field.

Facebook Groups: Many professional groups are active on Facebook, offering a platform to ask questions, share insights, and connect with peers.

Industry-Specific Forums and Websites: Joining forums related to your field can help you connect with peers and stay updated on industry trends.

Alumni Networks: Leverage your alma mater's network for connections. Alumni are often more willing to support and collaborate with fellow graduates.

Eventbrite: A resource for finding events, workshops, and seminars that you can attend to meet people in your industry.

Behance and Dribbble: For creatives, these platforms are not just for showcasing work but also for connecting with other designers and potential clients.

Real-Life Example

Alex, a Freelance Web Developer: Alex regularly attended tech meetups in his city, which he found through Meetup.com. Through these events, he not only stayed updated on industry trends but also met several of his long-term clients. He actively participated in discussions on LinkedIn and joined web development groups where he shared his insights and connected with potential clients.

Conclusion

Effective networking for freelancers is about finding the right balance between online and offline strategies. It involves actively engaging with your professional community, offering value, and consistently nurturing the relationships you build.

With the right approach, networking can open doors to numerous opportunities for growth and success in your freelancing career.

Collaboration and Community Engagement

Collaboration and community engagement are essential aspects of social development and organizational success. Here's a brief overview of each:

Collaboration Definition: Collaboration involves two or more people or organizations working together to achieve shared goals. It's a cooperative process where participants actively engage, share ideas, and leverage each other's strengths.

Benefits:

Enhanced Problem Solving: Diverse perspectives can lead to more creative and effective solutions.

Increased Efficiency: Pooling resources and expertise can lead to faster achievement of objectives.

Learning and Growth: Individuals can learn from each other, acquiring new skills and knowledge.

Challenges:

Communication Barriers: Differences in communication styles or lack of clarity can hinder progress.

Conflict: Differing opinions or competition can lead to disagreements.

Resource Allocation: Ensuring fair and effective use of shared resources can be complex.

Strategies for Effective Collaboration:

Clear Communication: Establish open, honest, and regular communication channels.

Defined Roles and Responsibilities: Clarify each participant's role to avoid confusion.

Foster Trust and Respect: Encourage a culture of mutual respect and trust.

Community Engagement

Definition: Community engagement involves actively involving community members in decision-making processes or initiatives that affect them. It's about building meaningful relationships with the community.

Benefits:

Improved Outcomes: Engaging those affected by decisions ensures that outcomes are more aligned with community needs.

Increased Trust: Transparency and involvement can build trust between organizations and communities.

Empowerment: Engagement empowers community members, giving them a voice in matters that concern them.

Challenges:

Diverse Opinions: Balancing differing viewpoints and interests can be difficult.

Resource Constraints: Effective engagement often requires time, money, and human resources.

Engagement Fatigue: Over-engaging or ineffective engagement strategies can lead to disinterest.

Strategies for Effective Community Engagement:

Inclusive Practices: Ensure that all community segments are represented and heard.

Continuous Feedback: Incorporate feedback mechanisms to understand community needs and perceptions.

Long-term Commitment: View engagement as an ongoing process, not a one-time event.

In summary, both collaboration and community engagement are dynamic processes that require thoughtful planning and execution. They are crucial for fostering inclusive, effective, and sustainable outcomes in various social and organizational contexts.

CHAPTER 6: NAVIGATING CHALLENGES

Common Freelancing Challenges and Solutions

Freelancing offers flexibility and autonomy but also comes with its own set of challenges. Understanding these challenges and their solutions can help freelancers navigate their careers more effectively.

1. Irregular Income

Further Explanation: Freelancers often face unpredictable payment schedules. This unpredictability can make budgeting and financial planning challenging.

Example: A freelance graphic designer might experience a surge of projects one month and very few the next. To manage this, they can save a portion of their income during peak months to cover expenses during slower periods.

2. Finding Clients

Further Explanation: Constantly searching for new clients is crucial but time-consuming. It involves marketing oneself and networking effectively.

Example: A freelance writer might use social media and content marketing to showcase their expertise. They can also attend industry networking events to meet potential clients.

3. Work-Life Balance

Further Explanation: Without a set schedule, freelancers might find themselves working odd hours, leading to a poor work-life balance.

Example: A freelance consultant might set office hours from 9 am to 5 pm and avoid work emails or calls outside these hours to ensure time for personal activities.

4. Time Management

Further Explanation: Juggling multiple projects with different deadlines requires effective time management to avoid missed deadlines and burnout.

Example: A freelance photographer might use a digital calendar to track project deadlines and allocate specific time blocks for editing, client meetings, and shooting sessions.

5. Client Relationships

Further Explanation: Navigating different client personalities and expectations can be challenging, especially when facing demanding or unclear clients.

Example: A freelance web developer could create a clear contract outlining project scope, timelines, and revision limits to manage client expectations from the start.

6. Lack of Benefits

Further Explanation: Freelancers miss out on traditional employee benefits, which can impact long-term financial planning and health security.

Example: A freelancer might join a professional organization that offers group health insurance rates. They could also set up a self-employed pension plan for retirement savings.

7. Skill Development

Further Explanation: Staying competitive requires keeping skills updated in a fast-evolving market, which requires ongoing education and adaptation.

Example: A freelance digital marketer could take online courses in the latest social media strategies and attend industry webinars to stay ahead in their field.

8. Legal and Financial Compliance

Further Explanation: Managing contracts, taxes, and invoices can be complex, requiring a good understanding of legal and financial practices.

Example: A freelance consultant might use invoicing software for billing and hire an accountant during tax season to ensure compliance and optimize tax deductions.

9. Isolation

Further Explanation: Working alone, primarily from home, can lead to social isolation and lack of collaboration opportunities.

Example: A freelance illustrator might join a local co-working space to interact with other professionals and participate in community events or online forums to stay connected.

10. Project Scarcity or Overload

Further Explanation: Balancing workload can be tricky; too few projects result in financial stress, while too many can lead to burnout.

Example: In times of low workload, a freelance videographer might offer promotional discounts or explore new markets. During high workload periods, they could outsource editing tasks to manage the volume effectively.

By addressing these challenges with specific strategies and examples, freelancers can navigate their careers more effectively, maintaining both their professional success and personal well-being.

Balancing Work and Personal Life

Balancing work and personal life as a freelancer can be challenging due to the flexible yet often unpredictable nature of freelance work. Here are strategies to help maintain this balance:

1. Set Fixed Work Hours

Strategy: Establish a regular work schedule and stick to it

Benefit: Creates a routine and separates work from personal time.

Example: A freelance graphic designer might decide to work from 9 am to 5 pm, Monday to Friday, mimicking a traditional work schedule.

2. Create a Dedicated Workspace

Strategy: Have a specific area in your home designated for work.

Benefit: Helps mentally shift into work mode and keeps work separate from personal life.

Example: Setting up a home office or even a designated corner with a desk and necessary equipment can create a work-conducive environment.

3. Use Time Management Tools

Strategy: Implement tools like digital calendars, project management apps, or time-tracking software.

Benefit: Keeps track of deadlines and helps prioritize tasks efficiently.

Example: Using apps like Trello for project management or Google Calendar for scheduling can help organize and visualize workloads.

4. Prioritize Self-Care

Strategy: Schedule regular breaks and prioritize activities that promote well-being.

Benefit: Prevents burnout and maintains overall health.

Example: Taking short breaks every hour for stretching or a walk, and scheduling time for exercise, hobbies, or relaxation.

5. Learn to Say No

Strategy: Avoid overcommitting by turning down projects that don't fit into your schedule or align with your goals.

Benefit: Ensures manageable workload and quality output.

Example: Politely declining a project when your schedule is already full, rather than overloading yourself.

6. Set Boundaries with Clients

Strategy: Communicate your availability and stick to it.

Benefit: Manages client expectations and prevents work from spilling into personal time.

Example: Informing clients about your working hours and not responding to work communications outside these hours.

7. Plan and Prioritize Tasks

Strategy: Prioritize tasks based on urgency and importance.

Benefit: Improves productivity and ensures important tasks are not overlooked.

Example: Using the Eisenhower Box method to categorize tasks into urgent, important, less urgent, and less important.

8. Delegate or Outsource

Strategy: Delegate tasks to others or outsource when workload is too high.

Benefit: Reduces stress and workload, allowing focus on core competencies.

Example: Hiring a virtual assistant for administrative tasks or outsourcing tasks like accounting.

9. Regularly Review and Adjust

Strategy: Continuously assess work-life balance and make adjustments as needed.

Benefit: Ensures that neither work nor personal life is neglected.

Example: Periodically reviewing your work schedule and adjusting it based on current personal commitments or workload.

10. Connect with Other Freelancers

Strategy: Engage with a community of freelancers for support and advice.

Benefit: Provides a sense of community and valuable insights.

Example: Joining online forums, local freelancer meetups, or co-working spaces to interact with peers.

Implementing these strategies requires discipline and self-awareness, but they can significantly enhance the quality of both professional and personal life for freelancers. Balancing the two effectively leads to a more fulfilling and sustainable freelance career.

Managing Financial Uncertainty

Managing financial uncertainty, especially in the context of freelancing or irregular income streams, requires careful planning and strategy. Here are key approaches to help navigate these challenges:

1. Build an Emergency Fund

Strategy: Save a portion of your income to create a financial cushion for lean periods.

Importance: Provides a safety net during times of reduced income or unexpected expenses.

Example: Aim to save enough to cover at least 3-6 months of living expenses. For instance, if your monthly expenses are $2,000, strive to save $6,000 to $12,000.

2. Diversify Income Sources

Strategy: Develop multiple streams of income to reduce reliance on any single source.

Importance: Diversification reduces the risk of financial hardship if one income stream dries up.

Example: Alongside freelance work, consider part-time employment, passive income streams like rental income or investments, or side businesses.

3. Budgeting and Expense Tracking

Strategy: Keep a detailed budget and track all expenses.

Importance: Helps in understanding spending patterns and identifying areas where expenses can be reduced.

Example: Use budgeting apps or spreadsheets to categorize and monitor monthly expenses, and adjust spending habits accordingly.

4. Flexible Financial Planning

Strategy: Create a flexible financial plan that can adapt to changing income levels.

Importance: Allows for adjustments in spending and savings in response to fluctuating income.

Example: Have a basic budget for essential expenses and an extended budget for periods of higher income.

5. Invest in Skills and Education

Strategy: Continuously develop skills and education to enhance employability and income potential.

Importance: Increases competitiveness and the likelihood of securing higher-paying opportunities.

Example: Attend workshops, online courses, or obtain certifications in your field to stay relevant and open up new income opportunities.

6. Health and Disability Insurance

Strategy: Secure health and disability insurance to mitigate financial risks associated with illness or inability to work.

Importance: Protects against the high costs of healthcare and loss of income due to health-related work absences.

Example: Research and invest in an insurance plan that covers major health expenses and provides disability benefits.

7. Retirement Planning

Strategy: Regularly contribute to a retirement fund or savings plan.

Importance: Ensures financial security in later years, especially important for those without employer-sponsored retirement plans.

Example: Set up an IRA (Individual Retirement Account) or a similar retirement plan and contribute a fixed percentage of your income monthly or quarterly.

8. Manage Debt Wisely

Strategy: Avoid high-interest debt and prioritize paying off existing debts.

Importance: Reduces financial strain and interest expenses.

Example: If you have multiple debts, use strategies like the debt snowball or avalanche methods to pay them off efficiently.

9. Emergency Contingency Plan

Strategy: Have a plan for severe financial downturns, like cutting non-essential expenses or temporarily taking on additional work.

Importance: Prepares you to act quickly and effectively in a financial crisis.

Example: Identify which expenses can be immediately reduced or eliminated if income significantly drops, such as subscription services or luxury items.

10. Professional Financial Advice

Strategy: Seek advice from financial advisors for personalized financial planning.

Importance: Provides expert guidance tailored to your specific financial situation and goals.

Example: Consult with a financial advisor to create a comprehensive financial plan, including investments, taxes, and estate planning.

These strategies emphasize the importance of proactive planning, risk management, and continuous adaptation to the financial realities of freelancing or irregular income streams. By implementing these practices, individuals can better navigate financial uncertainty and achieve long-term financial stability.

CHAPTER 7: GROWTH AND EXPANSION

Scaling Your Freelance Business

Scaling a freelance business involves expanding your client base, increasing revenue, and potentially hiring others to help manage the workload. It requires strategic planning and execution. Here are key steps to consider:

1. Identify Your Niche

Strategy: Focus on a specific market or skill set where you excel and that is in demand.

Why It's Important: Specializing can set you apart from competitors and attract more targeted clients.

Example: A graphic designer might specialize in branding for small businesses or digital illustrations for educational content.

2. Build a Strong Portfolio

Strategy: Showcase your best work to demonstrate your skills and attract potential clients.

Why It's Important: A compelling portfolio is often the deciding factor for clients when choosing a freelancer.

Example: Develop a professional website with case studies, testimonials, and a gallery of your work.

3. Optimize Pricing Strategy

Strategy: Review and adjust your pricing to reflect your experience, expertise, and the value you deliver.

Why It's Important: Appropriate pricing ensures that you are compensated fairly and can sustainably grow your business.

Example: Instead of hourly rates, consider value-based pricing where you charge based on the value and results you provide to the client.

4. Invest in Marketing

Strategy: Use various marketing channels to promote your services, such as social media, content marketing, and networking.

Why It's Important: Effective marketing increases visibility and attracts new clients.

Example: Regularly post your work and industry insights on LinkedIn or Instagram to engage with potential clients.

5. Streamline Business Processes

Strategy: Automate and streamline administrative tasks like invoicing, scheduling, and client communication.

Why It's Important: Efficiency in operations allows you to focus more on billable work and less on administrative tasks.

Example: Use tools like QuickBooks for accounting, Calendly for scheduling, and Trello for project management.

6. Expand Your Offerings

Strategy: Diversify your services or offer additional value to existing services.

Why It's Important: Expanding services can attract a broader range of clients and increase revenue streams.

Example: A freelance writer could start offering content strategy consultations in addition to writing services.

7. Build a Network and Collaborate

Strategy: Network with other professionals and collaborate on projects to expand your reach.

Why It's Important: Networking can lead to referrals, partnerships, and new business opportunities.

Example: Joining professional groups or online communities related to your field to connect with potential collaborators.

8. Consider Hiring or Outsourcing

Strategy: As your workload increases, hire subcontractors or outsource certain tasks.

Why It's Important: Delegating work can help manage an increased workload and allow you to focus on core business activities.

Example: Hiring a virtual assistant to handle administrative tasks or a junior freelancer to manage smaller projects.

9. Focus on Client Relationships

Strategy: Build strong, long-term relationships with clients through excellent service and communication.

Why It's Important: Satisfied clients can lead to repeat business and referrals.

Example: Regular check-ins with clients, asking for feedback, and providing personalized services.

10. Continuously Learn and Adapt

Strategy: Stay updated with industry trends and continuously improve your skills.

Why It's Important: Adapting to market changes ensures your business remains relevant and competitive.

Example: Attending workshops, webinars, or taking courses related to your field of work.

Scaling a freelance business is a gradual process that involves not just acquiring more clients, but also improving operational efficiency, building a brand, and potentially growing a team. This approach ensures sustainable growth and long-term success in the freelance market.

Diversifying Income Streams

Diversifying income streams is a crucial strategy for freelancers to ensure financial stability and reduce the risk associated with relying on a single source of income. Here's how freelancers can diversify their income:

1. Offer Multiple Services

Strategy: Expand your range of services to cater to different client needs within your field.

Benefits: Attracts a wider client base and increases earning opportunities.

Example: A freelance writer could offer copywriting, content creation, and editing services, catering to different aspects of writing and publishing.

2. Develop Passive Income Streams

Strategy: Create products or resources that generate income over time without continuous effort.

Benefits: Provides a steady income flow alongside active freelance work.

Example: Creating and selling online courses, e-books, or stock photography.

3. Affiliate Marketing

Strategy: Earn commissions by promoting products or services related to your field.

Benefits: Leverages your existing audience or network for additional income.

Example: A freelance web developer might promote web hosting services or coding tools through their blog or social media channels.

4. Subcontracting

Strategy: Outsource excess work to other freelancers for a fee.

Benefits: Enables handling more projects without overloading your schedule.

Example: A graphic designer with more projects than they can handle might subcontract some work to trusted colleagues, managing and overseeing their work for clients.

5. Consulting or Coaching

Strategy: Offer expert advice or coaching services in your area of expertise.

Benefits: Utilizes your knowledge and experience to help others while generating income.

Example: An experienced marketing freelancer might offer consulting services to businesses looking to develop marketing strategies.

6. Participating in Workshops and Speaking Engagements

Strategy: Conduct workshops or speak at events and conferences.

Benefits: Provides income and enhances your professional reputation.

Example: A freelance photographer might conduct workshops on photography techniques or speak at industry conferences.

7. Content Monetization

Strategy: Monetize content through platforms like YouTube, blogs, or podcasts.

Benefits: Generates income through ads, sponsorships, or memberships.

Example: A freelance IT consultant might start a tech-related podcast and gain revenue through sponsorships and advertisements.

8. Product Sales

Strategy: Create and sell products related to your field of expertise.

Benefits: Offers a creative outlet and an additional revenue stream.

Example: A freelance artist could sell prints, merchandise, or original artwork online.

9. Investment Income

Strategy: Invest a portion of your earnings into stocks, bonds, or real estate.

Benefits: Potential for long-term financial growth and additional income sources.

Example: Allocating a portion of freelance income to a well-diversified investment portfolio.

10. Collaborations and Partnerships

Strategy: Partner with other businesses or freelancers for joint projects or ventures.

Benefits: Opens up new opportunities and markets for your services.

Example: Collaborating with a software development firm on a project that requires both development and design expertise.

Diversifying income streams helps freelancers mitigate the risks of income fluctuations and economic downturns. It also encourages continuous growth and learning in new areas, adding depth and resilience to a freelance career.Continuous Learning and Skill Development

#

CHAPTER 8: THE FUTURE OF FREELANCING

Emerging Trends and Opportunities

In the constantly evolving landscape of work and technology, several emerging trends and opportunities are shaping various industries. Keeping abreast of these trends is essential for professionals looking to stay competitive and capitalize on new opportunities. Here are some notable trends and opportunities:

1. Remote Work and Digital Nomadism

The rise of remote work and digital nomadism has created a host of new freelancing opportunities. This trend, significantly accelerated by the COVID-19 pandemic, has led to a more flexible and location-independent work culture. Here's an overview of the opportunities this trend presents for freelancers:

1. Global Client Base

Opportunity: Access to a worldwide market of clients.

How It Works: Leveraging online platforms and networking to connect with clients from different countries and industries.

Example: A freelance graphic designer in India could work with clients in Europe or North America, expanding their client base beyond local opportunities.

2. Diverse Project Exposure

Opportunity: Opportunity to work on a wide range of projects across various sectors.

How It Works: Remote work allows freelancers to take on projects that aren't limited by geographical boundaries.

Example: A freelance writer could work on a tech blog for a Silicon Valley startup, a travel guide for a European tourism company, and a social media campaign for an Asian NGO.

3. Flexible Working Hours

Opportunity: Ability to set your own schedule.

How It Works: Choosing work hours that suit your lifestyle or when you're most productive, regardless of the client's location.

Example: A freelance web developer might choose to work late at night, which could coincide with daytime in a client's timezone, offering real-time collaboration.

4. Location Independence

Opportunity: Freedom to work from anywhere.

How It Works: As long as there's reliable internet access, freelancers can work from different locations – be it from home, a café, or while traveling.

Example: A digital marketing consultant could work from a beach in Bali, a café in Paris, or their home office in Canada.

5. Reduced Overhead Costs

Opportunity: Lower business expenses compared to traditional office-based work.

How It Works: Savings on commuting, office attire, and other expenses associated with a physical workplace.

Example: A freelance editor avoids the cost of commuting and renting office space by working from their home studio.

6. Work-Life Balance

Opportunity: Better control over work-life balance.

How It Works: Flexibility in scheduling work around personal life, family, and travel.

Example: A freelance consultant can schedule work around their children's school hours or plan a work schedule that allows for extended travel.

7. Niche Specialization

Opportunity: Focus on niche areas of expertise that might not be available locally.

How It Works: Targeting specific industries or specializations that have a global demand.

Example: A software developer specializing in AI can offer their niche skills to tech companies worldwide, even if local demand is limited.

8. Continuous Learning

Opportunity: Exposure to international standards and practices.

How It Works: Working with clients from different cultures and business environments encourages ongoing learning and adaptation.

Example: A project manager working with international teams learns about various project management methodologies and cultural communication styles.

9. Collaboration and Networking

Opportunity: Building a diverse professional network.

How It Works: Collaborating with other freelancers and professionals from around the world.

Example: A graphic designer might collaborate with a copywriter in another country for a branding project, expanding their professional network.

10. Higher Earning Potential

Opportunity: Potentially higher rates than local market.

How It Works: Charging rates that are competitive in international markets, which may be higher than what's typical in the freelancer's local market.

Example: A UX/UI designer in a developing country can earn more by working for clients in countries with higher market rates for these services.

Remote work and digital nomadism have not only transformed the landscape of freelancing but also expanded the horizons for freelancers to explore new opportunities, cultures, and work styles. This trend continues to grow, offering an ever-evolving array of prospects for those willing to adapt and embrace a more global, flexible work life.

Here are some example and resources for free lancing opportunity:

Example: Graphic designer in India working with clients globally.

Platform: Upwork (www.upwork.com) - A widely-used platform for freelancers across various fields to connect with global clients.

2. Diverse Project Exposure

Example: Writer working on varied international projects.

Platform: Freelancer (www.freelancer.com) - Offers a range of project types from clients around the world.

3. Flexible Working Hours

Example: Web developer working in different time zones.

Platform: Toptal (www.toptal.com) - Focuses on connecting top freelance developers with clients, offering flexibility in work hours.

4. Location Independence

Example: Digital marketing consultant working from different locations.

Platform: Fiverr (www.fiverr.com) - Ideal for freel

5. Reduced Overhead Costs

Example: A freelance editor working from a home studio could find editing projects on FlexJobs (www.flexjobs.com), a site specializing in remote and flexible job listings.

6. Work-Life Balance

Example: A freelance consultant planning work around personal commitments might use PeoplePerHour (www.peopleperhour.com), which allows freelancers to find projects fitting their schedule.

7. Niche Specialization

Example: A software developer specializing in AI can explore opportunities on GitHub Jobs (jobs.github.com), where tech companies post specialized project needs.

8. Continuous Learning

Example: A project manager seeking international exposure could find relevant projects on LinkedIn Freelance Marketplace (www.linkedin.com), leveraging its vast professional network.

9. Collaboration and Networking

Example: A graphic designer seeking collaborations can connect with copywriters on Behance (www.behance.net), which is popular among creative professionals.

10. Higher Earning Potential

Example: A UX/UI designer seeking higher rates might use Dribbble Jobs (jobs.dribbble.com), where design-focused companies look for top talent.

These platforms are well-suited for freelancers looking to capitalize on the opportunities presented by remote work and digital nomadism, offering a variety of projects and the flexibility to work from anywhere.

2. Artificial Intelligence and Automation

The integration of Artificial Intelligence (AI) and automation into various industries presents significant opportunities for freelancers. Here's how AI and automation are creating new freelancing niches and how one can capitalize on these trends:

Opportunities in AI and Automation for Freelancers:
AI and Machine Learning Development

Nature of Work: Developing and programming AI algorithms and machine learning models.

Skills Needed: Proficiency in programming languages like Python, expertise in machine learning libraries, and understanding of AI concepts.

Freelancing Platforms: Toptal (www.toptal.com) and Upwork (www.upwork.com) are popular for finding high-level development projects.

Data Science and Analytics

Nature of Work: Analyzing large datasets to derive actionable insights using AI tools.

Skills Needed: Data analysis, statistical skills, and proficiency in data science tools like R or Python's data-centric libraries.

Freelancing Platforms: Freelancer (www.freelancer.com) and Kaggle (www.kaggle.com) for data science competitions and projects.

AI-Driven Content Creation

Nature of Work: Using AI tools for content creation, such as automated writing, video production, or graphic design.

Skills Needed: Creative skills augmented with knowledge of AI-based content tools.

Freelancing Platforms: Fiverr (www.fiverr.com) and PeoplePerHour (www.peopleperhour.com) offer a variety of content creation gigs.

AI Integration Consulting

Nature of Work: Advising businesses on integrating AI into their operations.

Skills Needed: Knowledge of AI applications in business, strategic planning, and problem-solving skills.

Freelancing Platforms: LinkedIn Freelance Marketplace (www.linkedin.com) is a good place for professional consulting opportunities.

Chatbot Development and Training

Nature of Work: Creating and training chatbots for customer service, sales, or informational purposes.

Skills Needed: Programming skills, understanding of natural language processing, and conversational AI.

Freelancing Platforms: Upwork and Guru (www.guru.com) are popular for technical projects like chatbot development.

Automated Testing and Quality Assurance

Nature of Work: Using automation tools to test software and systems for bugs and performance issues.

Skills Needed: Knowledge of automated testing frameworks and software development lifecycle.

Freelancing Platforms: You can find QA testing projects on platforms like Upwork and Freelancer.

AI-Powered Marketing and SEO

Nature of Work: Leveraging AI tools for market analysis, SEO optimization, and personalized marketing strategies.

Skills Needed: Understanding of marketing principles, SEO, and AI-based marketing tools.

Freelancing Platforms: Hubstaff Talent (talent.hubstaff.com) and Fiverr are platforms where such skills are in demand.

AI-Enabled UX/UI Design

Nature of Work: Designing user interfaces and experiences using AI to analyze user data and preferences.

Skills Needed: UX/UI design skills combined with an understanding of AI's role in user experience.

Freelancing Platforms: Dribbble Jobs (jobs.dribbble.com) and Behance are great for creative design projects.

Maximizing Opportunities in AI and Automation:

Continuous Learning: Stay updated with the latest developments in AI and automation. Online courses and webinars can be instrumental in this.

Networking: Engage with AI and tech communities online and offline. Platforms like LinkedIn and tech meetups can be valuable.

Building a Portfolio: Work on projects that showcase your AI and automation skills. Personal projects, open-source contributions, or small freelance gigs can build an impressive portfolio.

Specialization: Choose a niche within AI and automation where you can build deep expertise.

The rapid advancement in AI and automation technologies means that these fields are continually evolving. Freelancers who are adaptable, continuously learn, and keep pace with technological advancements can find lucrative and fulfilling opportunities in this domain.

3. Green Economy and Sustainability

The growing focus on the green economy and sustainability offers diverse freelancing opportunities. As businesses and consumers increasingly prioritize environmental responsibility, freelancers can capitalize on this trend by offering services that support sustainable practices. Here are some potential freelance niches within this area:

1. Sustainable Business Consulting

Nature of Work: Advising businesses on how to implement sustainable practices in their operations, supply chain, and product development.

Skills Needed: Knowledge of sustainable business practices, environmental regulations, and corporate social responsibility (CSR).

Platforms: LinkedIn Freelance Marketplace (www.linkedin.com) and Upwork (www.upwork.com) are suitable for finding consulting projects.

2. Environmental Content Writing and Communication

Nature of Work: Creating content focused on sustainability topics, such as articles, reports, or social media content for eco-friendly brands.

Skills Needed: Strong writing skills and a good understanding of environmental issues and sustainability trends.

Platforms: Freelancer (www.freelancer.com) and Fiverr (www.fiverr.com) offer opportunities for content creation gigs.

3. Green Web Design and IT Services

Nature of Work: Offering web design and IT services that prioritize energy efficiency, minimal digital footprint, and use of sustainable resources.

Skills Needed: Web design and IT skills, with a focus on energy-efficient coding practices and sustainable web hosting solutions.

Platforms: PeoplePerHour (www.peopleperhour.com) and Guru (www.guru.com) can connect you with clients seeking eco-friendly web solutions.

4. Eco-Friendly Graphic Design

Nature of Work: Designing with sustainability in mind, using eco-friendly materials and processes for print and digital media.

Skills Needed: Graphic design skills coupled with knowledge of sustainable materials and processes.

Platforms: Behance (www.behance.net) and Dribbble Jobs (jobs.dribbble.com) are platforms where designers can showcase their sustainable design portfolios.

5. Sustainable Event Planning

Nature of Work: Organizing events, from conferences to weddings, with a focus on sustainability, such as zero waste, eco-friendly venues, and local sourcing.

Skills Needed: Event planning skills with a strong understanding of sustainable practices.

Platforms: Upwork and Eventbrite's event planning community can be good starting points for finding such opportunities.

6. Green Marketing and Social Media Management

Nature of Work: Specializing in marketing for sustainable brands, including social media management, eco-focused campaigns, and green product launches.

Skills Needed: Marketing skills with an understanding of eco-conscious consumer trends and green branding.

Platforms: Hubstaff Talent (talent.hubstaff.com) and FlexJobs (www.flexjobs.com) for remote marketing roles.

7. Eco-Consultancy for Homes and Offices

Nature of Work: Providing consultancy services for making homes and office spaces more energy-efficient and environmentally friendly.

Skills Needed: Knowledge of eco-friendly building practices, energy efficiency, and sustainable materials.

Platforms: Thumbtack (www.thumbtack.com) and Houzz (www.houzz.com) for local consultancy gigs.

8. Environmental Research and Data Analysis

Nature of Work: Conducting research and analyzing data related to environmental science, sustainability metrics, and green technologies.

Skills Needed: Research skills, proficiency in data analysis tools, and knowledge of environmental science.

Platforms: Academic freelance platforms and research institutions often post such opportunities.

Tips to Maximize Opportunities in Green Economy and Sustainability:

Stay Informed: Keep up-to-date with the latest trends, regulations, and innovations in sustainability and the green economy.

Build a Green Portfolio: Showcase projects or work that highlight your commitment and expertise in sustainability.

Network: Engage with sustainability-focused groups, online forums, and professional networks.

Offer Unique Solutions: Develop unique service offerings that address specific sustainability challenges in various industries.

Freelancers specializing in sustainability can not only find a range of opportunities across different sectors but also contribute to a more sustainable future. This field is expected to grow as more companies and individuals seek to reduce their environmental impact and embrace greener practices.

4. The Gig Economy and Freelance Platforms

The gig economy and freelance platforms have become increasingly pivotal in shaping the modern workforce. They offer flexible work arrangements and access to a global pool of talent and opportunities. Here's an overview of how these platforms are influencing the freelancing landscape:

The Rise of the Gig Economy

Definition: The gig economy refers to a labor market characterized by the prevalence of short-term contracts or freelance work, as opposed to permanent jobs.

Impact on Freelancers: Provides flexibility and autonomy, allowing individuals to choose when, where, and how much they want to work.

Challenges: Lack of job security, benefits, and consistent income can be issues for those relying solely on gig work.

Key Features of Freelance Platforms

Access to a Global Market: Platforms connect freelancers with clients from all over the world, breaking down geographical barriers to employment.

Diverse Opportunities: They cater to a wide range of skills and industries, from writing and graphic design to web development and consulting.

Streamlined Work Processes: Many platforms offer tools for invoicing, communication, time tracking, and project management, simplifying the freelance workflow.

Feedback and Reputation Systems: Ratings and reviews help freelancers build credibility and trust with potential clients.

Popular Freelance Platforms and Their Specialties

Upwork (www.upwork.com)

Specialty: Offers a broad range of categories from web development to customer service.

Unique Feature: Provides a robust system for time tracking and client communication.

Fiverr (www.fiverr.com)

Specialty: Known for creative and digital services, including graphic design, digital marketing, and video editing.

Unique Feature: Gigs are productized, making it easy for clients to purchase services.

Freelancer (www.freelancer.com)

Specialty: Hosts a variety of freelance jobs, including writing, programming, and design.

Unique Feature: Features competitive bidding for projects.

Toptal (www.toptal.com)

Specialty: Focuses on connecting clients with the top 3% of freelance talent in software development, finance, and project management.

Unique Feature: Rigorous screening process to ensure quality.

PeoplePerHour (www.peopleperhour.com)

Specialty: Offers a range of services, including web development, writing, and marketing.

Unique Feature: Enables freelancers to send custom proposals to potential clients.

Behance (www.behance.net)

Specialty: Ideal for creatives looking to showcase their portfolios in design, photography, and illustration.

Unique Feature: Portfolio-centric platform, attracting clients looking for high-quality creative work.

Maximizing Opportunities in the Gig Economy

Building a Strong Profile: A compelling profile with a professional portfolio, detailed service descriptions, and client testimonials can significantly increase job prospects.

Networking and Community Engagement: Active participation in platform communities and networking can lead to more job referrals and collaborations.

Continuous Skill Development: Staying updated with industry trends and continuously enhancing skills are vital to remain competitive.

Diversifying Income Sources: Leveraging multiple platforms or combining gig work with other income streams can provide financial stability.

The gig economy and freelance platforms are reshaping the workforce landscape, providing freelancers with unprecedented flexibility and opportunity. However, success in this arena requires strategic planning, continuous learning, and effective self-marketing..

5. Online Learning and E-Education

The surge in online learning and e-education has opened up a wealth of opportunities for freelancers in various fields. This trend has been accelerated by technological advancements and the global shift to remote learning and training due to factors like the COVID-19 pandemic. Here's how freelancers can tap into this burgeoning market:

1. Course Creation and Instruction

Nature of Work: Developing and teaching online courses in your area of expertise.

Skills Needed: Expert knowledge in a specific subject, ability to create engaging content, and teaching skills.

Platforms: Udemy (www.udemy.com), Coursera (www.coursera.org), and Teachable (www.teachable.com) are popular for hosting and selling online courses.

2. Educational Content Writing and Development

Nature of Work: Writing and developing educational content, such as e-books, course materials, and study guides.

Skills Needed: Strong writing skills, subject matter expertise, and understanding of educational principles.

Platforms: Upwork (www.upwork.com) and Freelancer (www.freelancer.com) are good places to find content writing projects in education.

3. E-Learning Platform Technical Support

Nature of Work: Providing technical development and support for e-learning platforms, such as Learning Management Systems (LMS).

Skills Needed: IT and technical skills, familiarity with e-learning software and platforms.

Platforms: Guru (www.guru.com) and FlexJobs (www.flexjobs.com) offer listings for technical roles in e-learning.

4. Educational App Development

Nature of Work: Developing educational apps and games that aid learning for various age groups and subjects.

Skills Needed: App development skills, understanding of educational needs and gamification techniques.

Platforms: Toptal (www.toptal.com) and PeoplePerHour (www.peopleperhour.com) are platforms where you can find app development projects.

5. Online Tutoring and Coaching

Nature of Work: Providing one-on-one tutoring or coaching sessions online.

Skills Needed: Expertise in a specific subject, teaching skills, and the ability to engage students virtually.

Platforms: VIPKid (www.vipkid.com) and Chegg Tutors (www.chegg.com/tutors) are popular for online tutoring jobs.

6. Instructional Design

Nature of Work: Designing educational courses and materials that are effective and engaging in an online format.

Skills Needed: Knowledge of instructional design theories, course development tools, and creative skills.

Platforms: LinkedIn Freelance Marketplace (www.linkedin.com) and Indeed (www.indeed.com) often have listings for instructional design work.

7. Translation and Localization of Educational Content

Nature of Work: Translating educational content and adapting it to different languages and cultural contexts.

Skills Needed: Proficiency in multiple languages and an understanding of cultural nuances in educational content.

Platforms: ProZ (www.proz.com) and TranslatorsCafe (www.translatorscafe.com) are platforms dedicated to translation work.

Tips for Success in Online Learning and E-Education Freelancing:

Stay Updated: Keep abreast of the latest trends in e-education and online learning technologies.

Build a Portfolio: Showcase your previous work or projects to attract potential clients or employers.

Network: Connect with other education professionals and potential clients through social media, professional networks, and education conferences.

Quality Matters: In education, the quality and accuracy of content are paramount. Ensure that your work meets high educational standards.

The field of online learning and e-education offers diverse opportunities for freelancers, from content creation to technical support and app development. With the increasing demand for remote and flexible learning solutions, skilled professionals in this field are in high demand. **6. Mental Health and Well-being Focus**

The growing focus on mental health and well-being has created a unique niche in the freelancing world. As awareness and acceptance of mental health issues increase, there is a rising demand for services and content centered around this theme. Here's how freelancers can tap into this market:

1. Mental Health Writing and Blogging

Nature of Work: Creating content related to mental health, wellness, and self-care.

Skills Needed: Strong writing skills, knowledge of mental health topics, and the ability to write empathetically and informatively.

Platforms: Upwork (www.upwork.com) and Freelancer (www.freelancer.com) offer opportunities for content creation and blogging in this niche.

2. Wellness Coaching or Counseling

Nature of Work: Providing online coaching or counseling services focused on mental well-being, stress management, and lifestyle coaching.

Skills Needed: Qualifications in psychology, counseling, or life coaching; good interpersonal and communication skills.

Platforms: BetterHelp (www.betterhelp.com) and Talkspace (www.talkspace.com) connect mental health professionals with clients for online therapy.

3. Mindfulness and Meditation Training

Nature of Work: Conducting online sessions or creating content related to mindfulness, meditation, and relaxation techniques.

Skills Needed: Experience and knowledge in mindfulness practices, ability to guide meditation sessions.

Platforms: Insight Timer (www.insighttimer.com) and YouTube are popular for sharing meditation and mindfulness content.

4. Mental Health Advocacy and Public Speaking

Nature of Work: Speaking engagements, webinars, or workshops on topics related to mental health awareness.

Skills Needed: Public speaking skills, deep knowledge of mental health issues, and the ability to engage and educate audiences.

Platforms: LinkedIn (www.linkedin.com) can be used to network and find speaking opportunities.

5. Health and Wellness Podcasting or Vlogging

Nature of Work: Creating podcasts or video blogs focusing on mental health, wellness, and healthy living.

Skills Needed: Skills in audio or video production, content creation, and a charismatic online presence.

Platforms: Spotify for Podcasters (podcasters.spotify.com) and YouTube can host podcasts and vlogs.

6. Developing Mental Health Apps

Nature of Work: Designing and developing mobile applications that promote mental health and well-being.

Skills Needed: App development skills, understanding of user experience, and knowledge of mental health principles.

Platforms: Freelancer and Toptal (www.toptal.com) are platforms where you can find app development projects.

7. Online Fitness Training

Nature of Work: Providing virtual fitness training with a focus on mental health benefits such as stress reduction and mood improvement.

Skills Needed: Fitness training certification, knowledge of how physical activity benefits mental health.

Platforms: Trainerize (www.trainerize.com) and Zoom for conducting online training sessions.

Tips for Success in Mental Health and Well-being Freelancing:

Stay Credible: If providing advice or counseling, ensure you have the necessary qualifications and stay informed about the latest research and trends in mental health.

Be Sensitive: Mental health topics require sensitivity and understanding. It's important to approach these subjects with empathy and respect.

Promote Positively: Use your platform to promote positive mental health and well-being practices.

Network and Collaborate: Engage with mental health professionals, wellness communities, and influencers to expand your reach and impact.

The increasing focus on mental health and well-being offers freelancers a chance to make a meaningful impact while pursuing work in a field that is both challenging and rewarding. As this sector continues to grow, the demand for skilled professionals offering services and content in this area is likely to increase as well.

7. Blockchain and Cryptocurrency

The blockchain and cryptocurrency sectors have experienced significant growth and are rapidly evolving, offering numerous freelancing opportunities. This industry not only involves technical roles related to blockchain development and cryptocurrency trading but also encompasses a variety of support services and content creation roles. Here's a look at some potential freelancing opportunities in this space:

1. Blockchain Development

Nature of Work: Developing decentralized applications (dApps), smart contracts, and blockchain protocols.

Skills Needed: Proficiency in blockchain platforms like Ethereum, coding skills in Solidity, and understanding of decentralized ledger technology.

Platforms: Toptal (www.toptal.com) and Upwork (www.upwork.com) are known for high-level development projects, including blockchain.

2. Cryptocurrency Content Writing

Nature of Work: Writing articles, blogs, and whitepapers on topics related to cryptocurrency and blockchain technology.

Skills Needed: Strong writing skills, a good understanding of cryptocurrency markets and blockchain technology.

Platforms: Freelancer (www.freelancer.com) and CryptoJobs (crypto.jobs) offer opportunities for writers specializing in the crypto sector.

3. Cryptocurrency Trading and Analysis

Nature of Work: Trading cryptocurrencies, conducting market analysis, and providing investment advice.

Skills Needed: Knowledge of cryptocurrency markets, trading experience, and analytical skills.

Platforms: Independent trading through platforms like Binance (www.binance.com) or offering analysis services on Upwork or Fiverr (www.fiverr.com).

4. Crypto Community Management

Nature of Work: Managing online communities for cryptocurrency projects, including social media, forums, and chat groups.

Skills Needed: Strong communication skills, knowledge of cryptocurrency, and community engagement strategies.

Platforms: Remote.co (www.remote.co) and AngelList (angel.co) often list community management jobs in crypto companies.

5. Blockchain Consulting

Nature of Work: Advising businesses on how to implement and leverage blockchain technology.

Skills Needed: In-depth knowledge of blockchain technology, strategic planning, and business acumen.

Platforms: LinkedIn Freelance Marketplace (www.linkedin.com) and Upwork are good for finding consulting opportunities.

6. Cryptocurrency Wallet and Exchange Development

Nature of Work: Developing secure digital wallets and cryptocurrency exchange platforms.

Skills Needed: Software development skills, understanding of cryptography, and blockchain security protocols.

Platforms: Guru (www.guru.com) and Upwork host various software development gigs, including those in the cryptocurrency realm.

7. Blockchain Legal and Regulatory Consulting

Nature of Work: Providing legal advice on matters related to cryptocurrency transactions and blockchain technology implementation.

Skills Needed: Legal expertise in blockchain technology, knowledge of financial regulations and compliance.

Platforms: Upwork and FlexJobs (www.flexjobs.com) can be sources for legal consulting roles in the blockchain space.

8. ICO and Tokenomics Strategy

Nature of Work: Assisting with Initial Coin Offerings (ICOs) and developing token economic models.

Skills Needed: Understanding of tokenomics, ICO strategy, and regulatory environment.

Platforms: Cryptocurrency-specific job boards like CryptoJobs can offer such niche opportunities.

9. Smart Contract Auditing

Nature of Work: Reviewing and auditing smart contracts to ensure they are secure and function as intended.

Skills Needed: Knowledge of smart contract development, experience in security and auditing practices.

Platforms: Freelancer and Upwork often have listings for smart contract auditing projects.

10. Cryptocurrency Graphic and Web Design

Nature of Work: Designing websites, logos, and marketing materials for cryptocurrency businesses.

Skills Needed: Graphic design skills, familiarity with the cryptocurrency industry's aesthetic and branding needs.

Platforms: Behance (www.behance.net) and Dribbble Jobs (jobs.dribbble.com) are great for creative design projects in the crypto space.

Maximizing Opportunities in Blockchain and Cryptocurrency:

Stay Updated: The blockchain and cryptocurrency field is fast-evolving, so staying informed about the latest trends and technologies is crucial.

Networking: Engage with the blockchain and crypto communities through forums, social media, and attending industry events.

Build a Portfolio: Showcase any relevant projects or work you've done in the blockchain and crypto space to attract clients and employers.

Understand Regulatory Aspects: Given the evolving regulatory landscape around blockchain and crypto, understanding these aspects can be a valuable skill.

8. Personal Branding and Influencer Marketing

Personal branding and influencer marketing have become significant aspects of the digital landscape, especially in the realm of freelancing. They revolve around building a strong, individual brand identity and leveraging that to influence and engage an audience. Here's how freelancers can utilize these concepts:

Personal Branding for Freelancers

Definition: Personal branding involves creating and promoting a professional image or brand of oneself. It's about establishing a reputation and identity that resonates with your target audience or clients.

Importance: In freelancing, personal branding helps differentiate yourself from competitors, attract the right clients, and build trust.

Strategies:

Develop a Unique Value Proposition (UVP): Clearly articulate what sets you apart from others in your field.

Consistent Online Presence: Maintain a consistent persona and professional image across all digital platforms, including social media, your personal website, and professional networks like LinkedIn.

Content Creation: Share insights, experiences, and knowledge related to your field through blogging, videos, or podcasts to establish authority and expertise.

Engagement: Actively engage with your audience and community, responding to comments, participating in discussions, and networking.

Influencer Marketing for Freelancers

Definition: Influencer marketing involves using individuals with a significant following or influence (influencers) to promote products, services, or brands.

Relevance for Freelancers: Freelancers can either become influencers in their niche or help brands in executing influencer marketing campaigns.

Opportunities:

Becoming an Industry Influencer: By creating valuable content and building a following in your niche, you can position yourself as an influencer. This status can open up opportunities such as sponsored content, brand partnerships, and speaking engagements.

Influencer Marketing Services: If you have skills in marketing, social media, or content creation, you can offer services to businesses looking to engage with influencers. This could include influencer outreach, campaign management, and content strategy.

Platforms and Tools for Building Personal Brand and Influencer Marketing

Social Media Platforms: Instagram, Twitter, LinkedIn, and TikTok are key platforms for building a personal brand and engaging in influencer marketing.

Content Creation Tools: Tools like Canva, Adobe Creative Suite, and video editing software can help create high-quality content for branding.

Blogging Platforms: WordPress, Medium, or personal websites for sharing insights and professional experiences.

Analytics Tools: Google Analytics, Hootsuite, and similar tools to track engagement and effectiveness of your branding and marketing efforts.

Tips for Success in Personal Branding and Influencer Marketing:

Authenticity: Maintain authenticity in your branding and marketing efforts. Authenticity resonates more with audiences and builds trust.

Niche Focus: Specialize in a specific area. A well-defined niche can attract more targeted and engaged followers.

Continuous Learning: Stay updated with the latest trends in your industry and in digital marketing.

Networking: Connect with other professionals and influencers. Collaborations can enhance visibility and credibility.

Personal branding and influencer marketing are powerful strategies for freelancers in the digital age. They not only help in attracting better opportunities but also in commanding higher rates for your services. Building a strong personal brand and possibly leveraging it for influencer marketing can significantly elevate a freelancer's career trajectory.

9. Cybersecurity and Data Privacy

The growing concerns over cybersecurity and data privacy have opened up significant freelancing opportunities. As businesses and individuals increasingly move their operations online, the demand for experts in cybersecurity and data privacy is on the rise. Here's how freelancers can tap into this market:

1. Cybersecurity Consulting

Nature of Work: Advising businesses on how to protect their digital assets and sensitive information from cyber threats.

Skills Needed: Deep knowledge of network security, threat analysis, and security protocols.

Platforms: Upwork (www.upwork.com) and Freelancer (www.freelancer.com) often have listings for cybersecurity consulting.

2. Penetration Testing and Vulnerability Assessment

Nature of Work: Conducting authorized simulated cyberattacks to evaluate the security of systems.

Skills Needed: Expertise in penetration testing tools and methods, understanding of various operating systems and network configurations.

Platforms: Hack The Box (www.hackthebox.eu) offers practical penetration testing experience, and Upwork provides a platform for freelance penetration testers to find work.

3. Data Privacy Consulting

Nature of Work: Helping businesses comply with data privacy laws and regulations like GDPR, HIPAA.

Skills Needed: Knowledge of data protection laws, risk assessment capabilities, and policy development skills.

Platforms: LinkedIn Freelance Marketplace (www.linkedin.com) and FlexJobs (www.flexjobs.com) are useful for finding freelance data privacy consulting roles.

4. Cybersecurity Content Writing

Nature of Work: Writing articles, blogs, whitepapers, and reports on cybersecurity trends and best practices.

Skills Needed: Strong writing skills and a solid understanding of cybersecurity topics.

Platforms: ProBlogger Job Board (jobs.problogger.net) and Contena (www.contena.co) can be good starting points for finding writing gigs in the cybersecurity niche.

5. Security Awareness Training

Nature of Work: Creating and delivering training programs for organizations to educate employees about cybersecurity threats and safe practices.

Skills Needed: Knowledge of cybersecurity, teaching or training skills, and content development.

Platforms: Teachable (www.teachable.com) for creating online courses, and LinkedIn for networking with potential clients.

6. Developing Security Software and Tools

Nature of Work: Building software solutions to enhance cybersecurity, such as firewalls, anti-virus programs, or encryption tools.

Skills Needed: Software development skills, knowledge of cybersecurity threats and countermeasures.

Platforms: GitHub for showcasing your software development projects and AngelList (angel.co) for connecting with startups and tech companies.

7. Incident Response and Forensic Analysis

Nature of Work: Assisting organizations in responding to cyberattacks and conducting forensic analysis to identify the source and extent of breaches.

Skills Needed: Skills in incident response, digital forensics, and understanding of legal implications.

Platforms: Upwork and Indeed (www.indeed.com) may offer opportunities for freelance incident responders and analysts.

8. Legal and Compliance Advisory

Nature of Work: Providing legal advice related to cybersecurity incidents and data breaches.

Skills Needed: Legal expertise in cybersecurity, knowledge of international and national cyber laws.

Platforms: Upwork and legal-specific freelance platforms like Lawclerk (www.lawclerk.legal) can be suitable for finding such opportunities.

Tips for Success in Cybersecurity and Data Privacy Freelancing:

Stay Updated: Continuously update your knowledge in the fast-evolving field of cybersecurity and data privacy.

Networking: Engage with professional groups and forums in cybersecurity to stay connected with industry trends and opportunities.

Certifications: Obtain relevant certifications (like CISSP, CISM, CEH) to boost credibility and showcase expertise.

Build a Portfolio: Showcase your experience and projects, especially if you have worked on significant cybersecurity initiatives or helped businesses in data privacy compliance.

Freelancers with expertise in cybersecurity and data privacy are well-positioned to benefit from the growing need for these services across all sectors. As digital threats evolve, the demand for skilled professionals in this field is likely to continue growing. **10. Virtual and Augmented Reality**

Trend: Advancements in VR and AR technologies, expanding beyond gaming into education, training, and commerce.

Opportunity: Developing VR/AR content or applications for various industries.

Impact: Creative and tech professionals can explore innovative uses of VR/AR in their fields.

Staying informed and adaptable to these trends can open up new avenues for growth and development. Professionals, especially freelancers and entrepreneurs, can leverage these trends to explore new markets, develop additional skills, and create novel solutions that cater to the evolving needs of the global market

Preparing for Long-Term Success

Preparing for long-term success, especially in a career or business, involves a combination of strategic planning, continuous learning, and adaptability. Whether you're a freelancer, entrepreneur, or professional, these principles can guide you towards sustainable success:

1. Set Clear Goals and Vision

Strategy: Define what long-term success looks like for you. Set specific, measurable, achievable, relevant, and time-bound (SMART) goals.

Importance: Clear goals provide direction and a benchmark to measure progress.

Example: If you're a freelancer, your long-term goal might be to establish a stable client base in a specific niche, or for a business, it could be reaching a certain revenue milestone in five years.

2. Continuous Learning and Skill Development

Strategy: Invest in ongoing education and skill development. Stay updated with industry trends and advancements.

Importance: Keeps you relevant and competitive in a fast-changing market.

Example: Regularly attending workshops, webinars, or taking online courses related to your field.

3. Financial Management and Diversification

Strategy: Practice effective financial management. Diversify income sources to mitigate risks.

Importance: Financial stability is crucial for enduring challenging periods and investing in growth opportunities.

Example: As a freelancer, this might mean having multiple clients or income streams and maintaining an emergency fund.

4. Networking and Building Relationships

Strategy: Cultivate a strong professional network and build meaningful relationships with peers, mentors, and clients.

Importance: Networking can lead to new opportunities, collaborations, and support.

Example: Joining professional associations, attending industry events, and participating in online forums related to your field.

5. Focus on Health and Well-being

Strategy: Prioritize physical and mental health. Ensure a work-life balance.

Importance: Personal well-being directly impacts productivity and satisfaction.

Example: Regular exercise, hobbies, and time off work can help maintain balance.

6. Adaptability and Resilience

Strategy: Cultivate adaptability to change and resilience in the face of challenges.

Importance: The ability to pivot and endure setbacks is crucial for long-term success.

Example: Being open to changing business strategies or career paths based on market demands and personal growth.

7. Effective Time Management

Strategy: Develop and maintain efficient time management practices.

Importance: Maximizes productivity and ensures progress towards goals.

Example: Using tools like digital calendars and task management apps to organize and prioritize work.

8. Strategic Planning and Execution

Strategy: Regularly plan and review your strategies. Be proactive in executing plans.

Importance: Strategic planning helps in making informed decisions and aligns daily activities with long-term goals.

Example: Creating a yearly plan with milestones and reviewing progress quarterly.

9. Building a Personal Brand

Strategy: Develop and nurture a personal brand that reflects your values, skills, and experiences.

Importance: A strong personal brand can open doors to new opportunities and establish credibility.

Example: Active presence on professional social media, speaking at events, or publishing articles in your area of expertise.

10. Seeking Feedback and Mentoring

Strategy: Regularly seek feedback and consider finding a mentor for guidance.

Importance: Feedback helps in identifying areas for improvement, and mentorship provides valuable insights and advice.

Example: Regularly asking for client feedback or engaging with a mentor in your industry.

Success is not just about achieving immediate goals but also about laying the foundation for continuous growth and stability. By incorporating these strategies into your career or business planning, you can better prepare for long-term success and fulfillment.

Evolving with the Freelance Economy

The freelance economy is dynamic and ever-evolving. To succeed in this landscape, freelancers need to adapt to changing trends and market demands. Here's how you can evolve with the freelance economy:

1. Embrace Remote Work

Trend: Remote work is becoming increasingly prevalent, and clients often seek freelancers who can work remotely.

Adaptation: Invest in a home office setup, improve your digital communication skills, and ensure a reliable internet connection.

2. Stay Updated with Technology

Trend: Technology and software tools evolve rapidly. Staying current is essential.

Adaptation: Continuously learn new tools and software relevant to your field, such as project management apps, design software, or coding languages.

3. Specialize and Niche Down

Trend: Clients value specialized expertise. Niche freelancers often command higher rates.

Adaptation: Identify your niche or specialty and focus on building your skills and reputation within it.

4. Diversify Income Streams

Trend: Relying on a single source of income can be risky. Diversification provides stability.

Adaptation: Explore complementary services or products you can offer to diversify your income.

5. Develop a Strong Online Presence

Trend: Clients often discover freelancers online. A robust online presence is crucial.

Adaptation: Maintain an updated website or portfolio, engage on social media, and use platforms like LinkedIn to showcase your work.

6. Networking and Building Relationships

Trend: Networking remains vital. Building relationships can lead to referrals and collaborations.

Adaptation: Attend virtual and in-person events, join professional groups, and foster connections with colleagues and clients.

7. Offer Value-Based Pricing

Trend: Clients are looking for value, not just low prices. Value-based pricing is gaining popularity.

Adaptation: Understand your clients' needs deeply and price your services based on the value you provide.

8. Embrace Automation

Trend: Automation tools can streamline tasks and improve efficiency.

Adaptation: Explore automation tools to handle repetitive tasks, such as invoicing, project management, or email responses.

9. Upskill and Reskill

Trend: Freelancers who continually learn and adapt to new skills remain competitive.

Adaptation: Invest in training and upskilling in areas that align with industry trends and client demands.

10. Seek Feedback and Reviews

Trend: Online reviews and client testimonials carry significant weight.

Adaptation: Encourage clients to provide feedback and reviews on platforms like Google, LinkedIn, or industry-specific websites.

11. Prioritize Mental Health and Well-being

Trend: Freelancers are recognizing the importance of mental health and work-life balance.

Adaptation: Implement self-care routines, set boundaries, and take breaks to maintain mental and emotional well-being.

12. Be Adaptable and Resilient

Trend: Economic and market uncertainties are common. Resilience is key.

Adaptation: Develop adaptability and resilience to navigate challenges and uncertainties effectively.

13. Legal and Contractual Awareness

Trend: Freelancers must be aware of legal and contractual aspects, including tax regulations.

Adaptation: Stay informed about relevant laws and consult legal professionals when necessary.

14. Environmental and Social Responsibility

Trend: Clients and consumers increasingly value environmentally and socially responsible freelancers and businesses.

Adaptation: Consider sustainability practices and responsible business operations.

By staying informed, continuously adapting, and remaining flexible, you can not only survive but thrive in the evolving freelance economy. Keep a pulse on industry trends and be proactive in adjusting your strategies to meet the changing demands of clients and the market.

CONCLUSION:

In conclusion, the freelance landscape offers a world of opportunities, but it also presents its unique set of challenges. To excel in freelancing, one must proactively address these challenges with strategic solutions. Here's a recap of key takeaways: Common Freelancing Challenges and Solutions: Freelancers can overcome challenges like income instability, client communication, and self-discipline by budgeting, using effective communication tools, and setting a routine.

Balancing Work and Personal Life: Achieving work-life balance involves setting boundaries, prioritizing self-care, and maintaining a flexible schedule.

Managing Financial Uncertainty: Freelancers can mitigate financial uncertainty by diversifying income sources, creating an emergency fund, and managing finances diligently.

Scaling Your Freelance Business: To scale, freelancers can specialize, outsource tasks, and market their services strategically.

Diversifying Income Streams: Diversification involves offering complementary services, creating passive income sources, and exploring new niches.

Emerging Trends and Opportunities: Staying updated with trends like blockchain, AI, and sustainability can lead to new opportunities for freelancers.

Freelancing in Remote Work and Digital Nomadism: Embracing remote work and digital nomadism can provide flexibility and a global client base.

Artificial Intelligence and Automation for Freelancing: Freelancers can leverage AI and automation to streamline tasks and improve efficiency.

Green Economy and Sustainability for Freelancing: Sustainability-focused freelancing can cater to eco-conscious clients and contribute to a greener future.

The Gig Economy and Freelance Platforms: Gig economy platforms offer diverse job opportunities, and freelancers should choose platforms that align with their skills and goals.

Online Learning and E-Education for Freelancing: Online learning and e-education provide avenues for freelancers to share knowledge and generate income.

Mental Health and Well-being Focus for Freelancing: Prioritizing mental health and well-being is essential for long-term success and work-life balance.

Blockchain and Cryptocurrency for Freelancing: Freelancers can tap into blockchain and cryptocurrency opportunities through development, content creation, and consulting.

Personal Branding and Influencer Marketing: Building a strong personal brand and engaging in influencer marketing can enhance visibility and credibility for freelancers.

Cybersecurity and Data Privacy for Freelancing: Freelancers can offer cybersecurity consulting, data privacy services, and content related to these crucial areas.

Preparing for Long-Term Success: Success planning involves setting clear goals, continuous learning, financial management, and building relationships.

Evolving with the Freelance Economy: Adapting to remote work, staying updated with technology, and specializing in niches are essential for freelance evolution.

The freelance landscape is ever-changing, and those who remain adaptable, resilient, and committed to self-improvement are best positioned to thrive in this dynamic environment. Whether you're a seasoned freelancer or just starting, these strategies can help you navigate challenges and build a successful freelance career. Some inspiring quotes:

Believe in Yourself: "Believe you can, and you're halfway there." - Theodore Roosevelt

Embrace Challenges: "In the middle of every difficulty lies opportunity." - Albert Einstein

Stay Curious: "The important thing is not to stop questioning. Curiosity has its own reason for existence." - Albert Einstein

Build a Support Network: "Surround yourself with only people who are going to lift you higher." - Oprah Winfrey

Celebrate Small Wins: "Success is not final, failure is not fatal: It is the courage to continue that counts." - Winston Churchill

Set Realistic Goals: "Goals transform a random walk into a chase." - Mihaly Csikszentmihalyi

Maintain Work-Life Balance: "The key is not to prioritize what's on your schedule, but to schedule your priorities." - Stephen R. Covey

Never Stop Marketing Yourself: "Your brand is what people say about you when you're not in the room." - Jeff Bezos

Adapt and Evolve: "It is not the strongest of the species that survive, nor the most intelligent, but the one most responsive to change." - Charles Darwin

Stay Persistent: "The difference between a successful person and others is not a lack of strength, not a lack of knowledge, but rather a lack in will." - Vince Lombardi

Remember Your "Why": "The two most important days in your life are the day you are born and the day you find out why." - Mark Twain

Stay Inspired: "Your work is going to fill a large part of your life, and the only way to be truly satisfied is to do what you believe is great work." - Steve Jobs

Trust the Process: "Success is a journey, not a destination. The doing is often more important than the outcome." - Arthur Ashe

You're Not Alone: "Alone, we can do so little; together, we can do so much." - Helen Keller

Enjoy the Ride: "Life is either a daring adventure or nothing at all." - Helen KellerCall to Action for Aspiring Freelancers

Appendix:

Additional Resources (Books, Websites, Communities)

Here are additional resources, including books, websites, and communities, that can provide valuable insights and support for freelancers:

Books:

"The Freelancer's Bible" by Sara Horowitz and Toni Sciarra Poynter - A comprehensive guide to freelancing, covering everything from financial management to marketing your services.

"Company of One: Why Staying Small Is the Next Big Thing for Business" by Paul Jarvis - Explores the benefits of building a successful freelancing business that doesn't require constant growth.

"The $100 Startup: Reinvent the Way You Make a Living, Do What You Love, and Create a New Future" by Chris Guillebeau - Offers practical advice on launching a small, profitable business with minimal investment.

"The Lean Startup: How Today's Entrepreneurs Use Continuous Innovation to Create Radically Successful Businesses" by Eric Ries - Provides insights on building a business or freelancing venture with a focus on experimentation and adaptability.

"Deep Work: Rules for Focused Success in a Distracted World" by Cal Newport - Explores strategies for achieving deep focus and productivity in your freelance work.

Websites:

Fiverr (www.fiverr.com) - A platform where freelancers can offer their services across various categories, from writing to design.

Guru (www.guru.com) - A freelancing platform that connects freelancers with clients seeking a wide range of services.

Toptal (www.toptal.com) - A network of top freelancers and experts in various fields, often catering to higher-end projects.

Freelance Writing Jobs (www.freelancewritinggigs.com) - A job board and resource hub specifically for freelance writers.

99designs (www.99designs.com) - A platform for designers to find freelance work, including graphic design, web design, and more.

PeoplePerHour (www.peopleperhour.com) - An online platform for finding freelance work in fields like web development, digital marketing, and content creation.

HubSpot Academy (academy.hubspot.com) - Offers free online courses in marketing, sales, and customer service, which can be valuable for freelancers.

The Freelancer's Guide (www.thefreelancersguide.com) -
A resource hub with articles, templates, and tools for freelancers
in various fields.

Becoming a Freelance Web Developer Blog
(www.becomeafreelancewebdeveloper.com) - Provides resources
and insights for aspiring freelance web developers.

Freelance Folder (www.freelancefolder.com) - A blog and
community for freelancers, offering articles and advice on
freelancing topics.

Communities:

Reddit Freelance (www.reddit.com/r/freelance) - A
subreddit where freelancers discuss their experiences, share
advice, and seek support from the freelance community.

Freelance Writers Den (www.freelancewritersden.com) -
A paid membership community specifically for freelance writers,
offering resources, forums, and training.

Freelance Folder Community
(www.freelancefolder.com/community) - An online community
of freelancers sharing tips, advice, and experiences.

LinkedIn Groups - Join relevant LinkedIn groups related
to your freelancing niche to connect with peers, share knowledge,
and discover opportunities.

Meetup (www.meetup.com) - Search for local freelance
or entrepreneurial meetups in your area to network with like-
minded professionals.

These resources can provide valuable support, guidance, and opportunities for freelancers looking to excel in their careers. Whether you're just starting or are a seasoned freelancer, exploring these books, websites, and communities can help you stay informed and connected in the freelancing world.

FAQs About Freelancing

Here are some frequently asked questions (FAQs) about freelancing along with concise answers:

1. What is freelancing?

Freelancing is a work arrangement where individuals offer their skills and services to clients or companies on a contract basis, typically for a specific project or period, without being employed full-time.

2. How do I get started as a freelancer?

To start freelancing, identify your skills and niche, create a portfolio showcasing your work, set competitive pricing, and start networking to find clients.

3. How do I find freelance clients?

You can find clients through freelancing platforms (e.g., Upwork, Freelancer), networking, social media, job boards, and referrals from your professional network.

4. What should I include in my freelance contract?

A freelance contract should specify project details, scope, deadlines, payment terms, revisions, and any legal aspects. It's essential for protecting both you and the client.

5. How do I determine my freelance rates?

Calculate your rates based on your skills, experience, market demand, and the value you provide. Research industry standards and adjust accordingly.

6. How do I manage my finances as a freelancer?

Keep track of income and expenses, create a budget, set aside taxes, and consider working with an accountant or using accounting software.

7. How can I ensure a steady income as a freelancer?

Diversify your income streams, maintain a consistent client pipeline, budget for lean months, and consider offering retainer agreements.

8. Is freelancing suitable for part-time work?

Yes, freelancing can be done part-time or full-time, depending on your availability and goals. Many freelancers start part-time and transition to full-time.

9. How can I improve my freelancing skills?

Continuous learning is key. Take online courses, read books, attend workshops, and practice your skills regularly to stay competitive.

10. What are the tax implications of freelancing?

- Freelancers are often considered self-employed. You may need to pay self-employment tax, set aside estimated taxes, and keep detailed financial records.

11. How can I handle client disputes or non-payment issues?

- Clearly define dispute resolution procedures in your contract. If issues arise, communicate with the client, document interactions, and consider legal action if necessary.

12. What are the benefits of freelancing?

- Freelancing offers flexibility, independence, the potential for higher income, and the opportunity to work on projects you're passionate about.

13. Are there downsides to freelancing?

- Challenges include income instability, self-employment taxes, lack of job security, and the need for self-discipline.

14. How can I stand out as a freelancer?

- Build a strong personal brand, provide exceptional service, deliver high-quality work, and maintain open and professional communication with clients.

15. What industries are suitable for freelancing?

- Almost any industry can have freelance opportunities. Common areas include writing, graphic design, web development, marketing, consulting, and more.

These FAQs cover some of the fundamental aspects of freelancing. Freelancing offers unique opportunities and challenges, and understanding these basics is crucial for success in this career path.

16. Is freelancing a stable career choice?

- Freelancing offers flexibility but can be less stable than traditional employment. Success depends on your ability to secure clients and manage finances.

17. How do I handle taxes as a freelancer?

- Freelancers often pay self-employment taxes, so it's essential to set aside a portion of your income for taxes. Consider consulting with a tax professional.

18. Can I freelance while working a full-time job?

- It's possible to freelance part-time while employed full-time, but be mindful of potential conflicts of interest and non-compete clauses in your employment contract.

19. What skills are in demand for freelancers?

- In-demand skills include web development, content writing, graphic design, digital marketing, programming, data analysis, and social media management.

20. How can I build a strong portfolio as a beginner freelancer?

- Start with personal projects or volunteer work, create sample pieces, and gradually build a portfolio that showcases your skills.

21. How do I handle project scope changes from clients?

- Clearly define the project scope in your contract, and if changes are requested, discuss them with the client and adjust the contract accordingly.

22. What is the difference between a freelancer and a contractor?

- Freelancers often work independently, while contractors may work for a company on a specific project. Both are usually hired on a temporary basis.

23. Should I specialize in one niche or offer a variety of services?

- Specializing can help you stand out, but offering a range of related services can attract more clients. Consider what aligns with your goals.

24. Can I negotiate my freelance rates with clients?

- Yes, negotiation is common in freelancing. Be prepared to discuss rates, project details, and deliverables to reach a mutually beneficial agreement.

25. How do I handle late payments from clients?

- Include payment terms and penalties for late payments in your contract. Follow up with reminders and consider legal action if necessary.

26. What insurance do I need as a freelancer?

- Consider liability insurance and professional indemnity insurance to protect yourself in case of legal disputes or errors in your work.

27. Are there online courses for freelancers?

- Yes, many platforms offer online courses and resources specifically tailored to freelancers to enhance their skills and knowledge.

28. What is the importance of networking as a freelancer?

- Networking helps you connect with potential clients, collaborators, and mentors. It can lead to valuable opportunities and referrals.

29. Can I work with international clients as a freelancer?

- Yes, freelancers often work with clients from around the world. Be mindful of time zones, payment methods, and any legal considerations.

30. How do I transition from freelancing to starting my own business?

- Transitioning to a business may involve registering as a legal entity, hiring employees, and scaling your operations. Seek legal and financial advice when making this shift.

Worksheets and Exercises for Planning and Goal Setting

Planning and goal-setting are essential for freelancers to stay organized and achieve success. Here are some worksheets and exercises that can help freelancers in their planning and goal-setting process:

**1. Freelance Business Plan Worksheet:

This worksheet guides freelancers in creating a business plan for their freelance ventures. It includes sections for defining your business goals, target audience, services offered, marketing strategies, and financial projections.

**2. SMART Goal-Setting Exercise:

Use the SMART (Specific, Measurable, Achievable, Relevant, Time-bound) criteria to set clear and achievable freelance goals. Write down your goals and ensure they meet each of the SMART criteria.

**3. Client Pipeline Tracker:

Keep track of potential clients, leads, and their status in your sales pipeline. This exercise helps you stay organized in your client acquisition efforts.

**4. Monthly Goal Tracker:

Create a monthly tracker to monitor your progress toward achieving your freelance goals. Record your goals, action steps, and results for each month.

**5. Income and Expense Tracker:

Maintain a detailed record of your freelance income and expenses. This exercise helps you manage your finances and plan for taxes.

**6. Marketing Strategy Planner:

Plan your marketing efforts by identifying your target audience, choosing marketing channels, setting a budget, and creating a content calendar.

**7. Client Project Planner:

For each client project, use this planner to outline project details, objectives, milestones, timelines, and budget.

**8. Time Management Worksheet:

Allocate your time effectively by tracking how you spend your work hours. Identify time-wasting activities and optimize your schedule.

**9. SWOT Analysis Worksheet:

Conduct a SWOT (Strengths, Weaknesses, Opportunities, Threats) analysis for your freelance business. Identify areas for improvement and potential growth opportunities.

**10. Networking and Collaboration Tracker:

- Keep a record of your networking activities, including events attended, contacts made, and potential collaborations. Networking is crucial for freelancers.

**11. Content Creation Planner:

- Plan your content creation efforts, including blog posts, social media content, and newsletters. This exercise ensures consistent content delivery.

**12. Feedback and Improvement Log:

- Document client feedback and your actions for improvement. Continuous improvement is essential for freelancers.

**13. Quarterly Business Review:

- Conduct a quarterly review of your freelance business. Reflect on achievements, challenges, and adjust your goals and strategies accordingly.

**14. Self-Assessment and Skills Development Plan:

- Evaluate your skills and identify areas for improvement. Create a plan for skill development through courses or practice.

**15. Freelance Budgeting Exercise:

- Create a budget for your freelance business, considering both business and personal expenses. This exercise helps you manage finances effectively.

End

www.ingramcontent.com/pod-product-compliance
Lightning Source LLC
Chambersburg PA
CBHW072155290526
45794CB00004B/1525